NOTES FOR PROFESSIONAL LIBRARIANS AND LIBRARY USERS

This is an original book title published by The Haworth Pastoral Press®, and imprint of The Haworth Press, Inc. Unless otherwise noted in specific chapters with attribution, materials in this book have not been previously published elsewhere in any format or language.

CONSERVATION AND PRESERVATION NOTES

All books published by The Haworth Press, Inc. and its imprints are printed on certified pH neutral, acid free book grade paper. This paper meets the minimum requirements of American National Standard for Information Sciences-Permanence of Paper for Printed Material, ANSI Z39.48-1984.

Peter A. Kahle, PhD
John M. Robbins, PhD

The Power of Spirituality in Therapy

Integrating Spiritual and Religious Beliefs in Mental Health Practice

Pre-publication REVIEWS, COMMENTARIES, EVALUATIONS . . .

"With *The Power of Spirituality in Therapy,* Kahle and Robbins join the vanguard of mental health professionals who boldly take on psychology's tradition of silence regarding spiritual issues. This work not only represents a challenge to therapy's God phobia, but it is also a highly personal, often bitingly funny, read. The authors' references range from Dennis Miller to Confucius, but they cleverly draw on the wisdom of many to strengthen their position. Of particular value are two chapters, 'The Power to Help' and 'The Power to Hurt,' which provide the clinician with thought-provoking questions for self-reflection. The concluding chapter wrestles with the merits of neutrality that therapists often hold forth as a preferred stance. Kahle and Robbins offer a convincing argument that religion and science are not in opposition, but that they are both helpful, and perhaps necessary, to clinical practice. The authors are to be commended for their boldness and transparency in leading the reader through this very personal and unsettling journey."

Delane Kinney, PhD
Director of Psychological Services, Salesmanship Club Youth and Family Centers

"This book will be welcomed especially by clergy who seek to refer members of their congregation for therapeutic help that is clinically sound and open to allow the resources of faith. The chapter on the integration of religion, spirituality, and clinical practice is very helpful in this regard."

Rev. Walter E. Waiser, MDiv
Senior Pastor, Peace Lutheran Church, Hurst, Texas

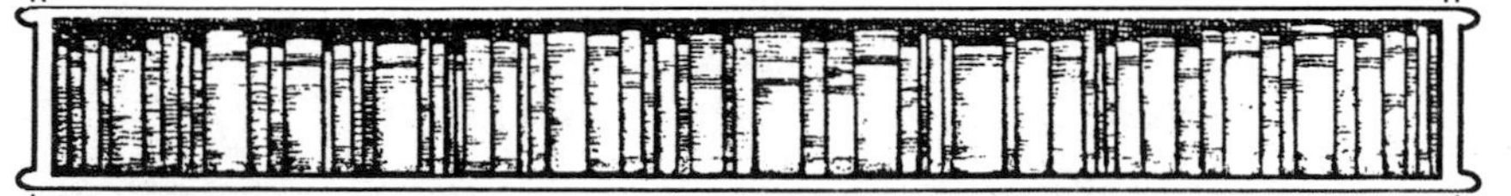

More pre-publication
REVIEWS, COMMENTARIES, EVALUATIONS . . .

"*The Power of Spirituality in Therapy* has been too long in coming to our field. I found the book inspiring and encouraging as a professional therapist, a trainer of therapists, and as a Christian. Somewhat in the style of C. S. Lewis or G. K. Chesterton, the book is like an apologetic for using 'God language' in therapy. Kahle and Robbins move us a step beyond the recent popularity of simply including 'spirituality' in therapy by integrating the Christian beliefs of clients as an ongoing part of therapy. This book brings the issue of spirituality and religion in therapy around to complete the circle of integration of therapy and spirituality."

Bonnie Osmon, PhD
Licensed Marriage and Family Therapist and Professional Counselor, AAMFT Approved Supervisor; Assistant Professor, Graduate Counseling and Biblical Studies: Family Studies, John Brown University

The Haworth Pastoral Press®
An Imprint of The Haworth Press, Inc.
New York • London • Oxford

The Power of Spirituality in Therapy

Integrating Spiritual and Religious Beliefs in Mental Health Practice

THE HAWORTH PASTORAL PRESS

Religion and Mental Health
Harold G. Koenig, MD
Senior Editor

The Obsessive-Compulsive Disorder: Pastoral Care for the Road to Change by Robert M. Collie

The Pastoral Care of Children by David H. Grossoehme

Ways of the Desert: Becoming Holy Through Difficult Times by William F. Kraft

Caring for a Loved One with Alzheimer's Disease: A Christian Perspective by Elizabeth T. Hall

"Martha, Martha": How Christians Worry by Elaine Leong Eng

Spiritual Care for Children Living in Specialized Settings: Breathing Underwater by Michael F. Friesen

Broken Bodies, Healing Hearts: Reflections of a Hospital Chaplain by Gretchen W. TenBrook

Shared Grace: Therapists and Clergy Working Together by Marion Bilich, Susan Bonfiglio, and Steven Carlson

The Pastor's Guide to Psychiatric Disorders and Mental Health Resources by W. Brad Johnson and William L. Johnson

Pastoral Counseling: A Gestalt Approach by Ward A. Knights

Christ-Centered Therapy: Empowering the Self by Russ Harris

Faith, Spirituality, and Medicine: Toward the Making of the Healing Practitioner by Dana E. King

Bioethics from a Faith Perspective: Ethics in Health Care for the Twenty-First Century by Jack Hanford

Family Abuse and the Bible: The Scriptural Perspective by Aimee K. Cassiday-Shaw

When the Caregiver Becomes the Patient: A Journey from a Mental Disorder to Recovery and Compassionate Insight by Daniel L. Langford and Emil J. Authelet

A Theology of God-Talk: The Language of the Heart by J. Timothy Allen

A Practical Guide to Hospital Ministry: Healing Ways by Junietta B. McCall

Pastoral Care for Post-Traumatic Stress Disorder: Healing the Shattered Soul by Dalene Fuller Rogers

Integrating Spirit and Psyche: Using Women's Narratives in Psychotherapy by Mary Pat Henehan

Chronic Pain: Biomedical and Spiritual Approaches by Harold G. Koenig

Spirituality in Pastoral Counseling and the Community Helping Professions by Charles Topper

Parish Nursing: A Handbook for the New Millennium edited by Sybil D. Smith

Mental Illness and Psychiatric Treatment: A Guide for Pastoral Counselors by Gregory B. Collins and Thomas Culbertson

The Power of Spirituality in Therapy: Integrating Spiritual and Religious Beliefs in Mental Health Practice by Peter A. Kahle and John M. Robbins

Bereavement Counseling: Pastoral Care for Complicated Grieving by Junietta Baker McCall

Biblical Stories for Psychotherapy and Counseling: A Sourcebook by Matthew B. Schwartz and Kalman J. Kaplan

A Christian Approach to Overcoming Disability: A Doctor's Story by Elaine Leong Eng

The Power of Spirituality in Therapy

Integrating Spiritual and Religious Beliefs in Mental Health Practice

Peter A. Kahle, PhD
John M. Robbins, PhD

The Haworth Pastoral Press®
An Imprint of The Haworth Press, Inc.
New York • London • Oxford

Published by

The Haworth Pastoral Press®, an imprint of The Haworth Press, Inc., 10 Alice Street, Binghamton, NY 13904-1580.

PUBLISHER'S NOTE
Identities and circumstances of individuals discussed in this book have been changed to protect confidentiality. Any resemblance to actual persons, living or dead, is entirely coincidental.

Cover design by Brooke R. Stiles.

Library of Congress Cataloging-in-Publication Data

Kahle, Peter A.
The power of spirituality in therapy : integrating spiritual and religious beliefs in mental health practice / Peter A. Kahle, John M. Robbins.
p. cm.
Includes bibliographical references and index.
ISBN 0-7890-2113-7 (alk. paper)—ISBN 0-7890-2114-5 (pbk. : alk. paper)
1. Psychotherapy—Religious aspects. I. Robbins, John M., 1966-II. Title.
RC489.S676K34 2003
616.89'14—dc21

2003001809

To God, thank you for your love, grace, mercy, wisdom, forgiveness, and for the gift of laughter. We thank you also for blessing our lives with two amazing women, Amber and Mary Ann, who have made our lives more enjoyable than we could have ever dreamed. Thank you also for the gift of human life you blessed us with during this project, Addison Nicole Kahle. Indeed, your grace endures forever.

ABOUT THE AUTHORS

Peter Kahle, PhD, is a licensed psychologist in the state of Texas who currently serves as Senior Counselor at the Dallas Campuses of the Texas Women's University Counseling Center in addition to working in his private practice, Crossways Counseling & Consulting, in Grapevine, Texas. He is also a faculty member of the Reunion Institute in Dallas. His writing has appeared in *101 More Interventions in Family Therapy* (Haworth) and in the *Journal of Systemic Therapies.*

John Robbins, PhD, is a licensed marriage and family therapist in private practice in North Carolina. He is the founder of the T.E.A.M.© Program, a therapeutic group for at-risk adolescents. His writing has appeared in *101 More Interventions in Family Therapy* (Haworth) and in the *Journal of Systemic Therapies.*

CONTENTS

Foreword

Spirituality has become an officially recognized hot topic in the mental health disciplines over the past several years, and for good reason. Workshops, journal articles, and a few books (the present one among them), are now available that explicitly address the issue. There are many reasons behind this development. First, many people seeking help view their lives in some kind of spiritual terms and welcome these terms into therapy. They often assume that their orientations to spiritual things (and their other values as well) are largely shared by their therapists, and so it makes sense to them that spirituality should or could be a legitimate realm for discussion and examination, and, ultimately, help. The fact that Americans more and more view therapists as sources of help alongside, or perhaps in place of or interchangeable with, clergy leads to a seemingly natural inclusion of spiritual concerns in therapeutic conversations.

Among practicing professionals, too, has come an increasing awareness of the need for examining foundational beliefs of clients as they attempt to live out their lives. As the field embraces diversity, a concern for considering worldview is completely appropriate, even if this is one aspect of diversity that has largely failed to show up on the larger professional radar screen. Indeed, as this book attests, it is the rare multicultural course that includes religiously or spiritually grounded worldviews in its examination to any significant degree. Finally, for professionals who have been including spirituality in their work, psychotherapy that ignores or downplays spirituality can take on the dryness of a desert. Dry therapy is rarely effective for the client and rarely energizing to the therapist.

By way of example, I recently had the opportunity to moderate a panel on spirituality at a major professional conference. The panel presentation's title was "Incorporating Spirituality into Marriage and Family Therapy." In my opening comments, I suggested that for many of us, it might be more accurate to say that we're interested in the reverse: incorporating marriage and family therapy into our spirituality. The response of the audience was large-scale and enthusiastic agreement. For many, there's a sense that "it's about time" the mental health profession began acknowledging the importance of the spiritual dimension of life. Therapy is not seen as just something that we do; it is part of who we are and part of what makes us fully alive and human.

At the same time, including spirituality in therapy is a development that makes a lot of people rather nervous. Spirituality is not usually one of the first things people think of when discussing mental health or behavioral science, unless they are coming from a religious perspective. The discipline of pastoral counseling comes to mind, but there are also many therapists who identify themselves as explicitly religious, with "Christian counselors" being the most obvious example. For those who do not identify with an "institutional" spiritual or religious perspective, however, there are few maps to follow for how to work in this area well. Without guidance, risks increase, and so do therapists' anxieties about it.

In addition, the topic of spirituality is very "soft" sounding, and those professionals who prefer the scientific end of the spectrum may tend to be a bit suspicious of the whole thing. Furthermore, psychology has traditionally been seen as less than friendly to religion (or so it has seemed), and spirituality sounds a lot like religion, even though there are many spiritually oriented therapists who strenuously differentiate between religion and spirituality.

Underneath it all, perhaps, is a concern about spirituality being turned into a professionally and therapeutically sanctioned prescriptive sledgehammer for any number of particular worldviews, religions, political ideologies, social causes, and/or therapists' personal agendas. The danger of this occurring is a very legitimate concern, but that alone does not justify dismissing spirituality as a whole. In fact, there is a very notable history within the field of how its public philosophy articulates a set of privileged, "healthy" values that therapists then are de facto encouraged to influence clients toward. This is in reality what we do—we influence people to think and act differently so that they can be more free to live life as they wish, within limits that recognize a social world in which we all must participate. The tension, then, exists in how to identify and work well within those accepted values while respecting clients' freedom to choose elsewise. What makes spirituality such a potentially frightening thing is that it is categorically wrapped up in foundational beliefs and values, and we don't know how to ask and answer questions in that arena on a level broad enough to socialize the profession to some kind of consensus.

Peter Kahle and John Robbins attempt to do just that, and much more, in this very timely and very readable book. *The Power of Spirituality in Therapy: Integrating Spiritual and Religious Beliefs in Mental Health Practice* is a groundbreaking yet eminently user-friendly text that should start a lot of conversations and generate much good thinking about the topic, as well as offer some guidance about actually doing good therapy around issues of spirituality. Rather than simply being a dry treatise on theory and conceptual knowledge targeted to academicians primarily, the authors take a decidedly different, much more applied and broad approach that will appeal to academicians, students, and "in-the-trenches" practitioners alike. Some practical potatoes are included along with the conceptual meat. The authors want folks to (1) examine their own assumptions personally and at a larger professional level, and (2) actually practice a bit differently (or at least more confidently and comfortably) when it comes to the foundational things on which spirituality readily draws.

They succeed on both counts. First, they make a very compelling and empirically based case for just how important it is that therapists be open to working with clients in the area of spirituality. They also point out how deficient the typically trained therapist is to do so. Throughout the course of the book, they articulate how therapists can include spirituality in a productive and sensitive, ethically responsible manner. This is definitely of practical value to the real-world therapist. Further, it is written from a warm and personal standpoint, and the authors make liberal use of personal anecdotes and humor to illustrate their points, and salient quotations from an exceedingly wide range of people, including Confucius, Freud, Dennis Miller, C. S. Lewis, Mother Teresa, and Clint Eastwood's Dirty Harry Callahan. It's a fun read!

That being said, it's important to include some notes of caution to the reader. What this book is *not* is a cookbook, how-to manual that gives you a menu of nifty techniques to plug into the session next Tuesday with the XYZ religious family, or the clients on Friday explicitly looking for spiritual or religious guidance. In fact, some readers might find this book a little frustrating because the counsel offered is not very specific in terms of actual things (i.e., spiritual interventions) to do with clients. But that is part of what comes with addressing this topic, and Kahle and Robbins are clear about that. They do not pretend to be offering the final authoritative perspective on spirituality but rather to bring some things to clear awareness and offer bold suggestions for managing those things well.

Second, the authors are not timid in offering their perceptions and opinions, and our profession's usually implicit, but occasionally explicit, assumptions about spirituality and religion are studiously examined and thoughtfully challenged. Fortunately, this is done in a gentle and respectful manner, although I have no doubt some will take significant offense at having their assumptions addressed in a way that is usually not done. In short, Kahle and Robbins unapologetically but gracefully are not politically correct. If you are looking for a wimpy, let's-all-just-get-along book, this one might not be for you.

That's a good thing, too, because spirituality (an acceptable term) and religion (a more suspicious term) are often intimately related, and they provide the substance from which our most deeply held beliefs and values are generated. In short, there are things worth fighting about, and these would be among them! If we are to help clients make changes and grow toward goals they and we collaboratively set, we must be willing to get down and wrestle in the axiological mud with them. In order to do this, we must first do this among ourselves, and Kahle and Robbins offer us a substantive starting point from which to begin. We will not end up in full agreement within the field, but we as a whole will be better prepared to assist those seeking our help.

Mark Odell, PhD
University of Nevada, Las Vegas

Acknowledgments

We want to give special thanks first and foremost to our beautiful wives, Amber and Mary Ann. The support, encouragement, and patience they showed us throughout this process are appreciated more than they'll ever know. They continue to inspire us every day.

We greatly appreciate our lovely parents, Ray and Bonnie Kahle and J. M. and Laura Robbins. We thank them for raising us in Christian homes and instilling in us the importance of faith. We thank them for practicing the Christian principles of grace and mercy . . . for undoubtedly, we know we tested their faith and patience more times than we would like to remember. We'd also like to thank all of our other family members. On my side (PK), I wish to thank David, Susan, Karen, Jason, Austin, Kearsten, Walt, Vonnie, Patrick, Heather, and Hannah. On my side (JR), I wish to thank Ray, Mike, Tom, and LaNelle. We thank them, and all those who are a part of their lives, for their support, encouragement, and patience as our work, unfortunately, made us less available at times than we would have liked. We love them all very much!

We would especially like to recognize the encouragement we received from two family members who specifically encouraged us to write this book. We thank Ray for modeling courage and wisdom related to addressing spiritual and religious issues in his own training, both in graduate and postgraduate training. We offer thanks to him for also helping us to notice some of the subtle contradictions within the popular philosophies of the day. For example, the contradictory assertion that contradictions in philosophical thought are irrelevant. We thank Tom for his unwavering encouragement, dare we say supportive directive, to put our humorous musings down on paper. His matter-of-fact approach made it quite clear to us that the only thing he questioned in our thinking was why we would even bother questioning whether this book should be written.

We thank the very talented and gifted Andrew Kendall. His artistic creativity and expertise, along with his educational background in religious studies and philosophy, were invaluable in capturing the essence of what we were articulating with words through the medium of art. We thank the gifted Dr. Mark Odell for his willingness to share his gifts with our readers through the Foreword. We also thank our gifted colleagues who agreed to be readers in this project: Reverend Raymond Kahle, Reverend Walter Waiser, Dr. Bonnie Osmon, Dr. Delane Kinney, Dr. Rick Fowler, Dr. Tom Smith, and Melissa Elliott.

Thanks also go out to Dr. Linda Rubin, Dr. Basil Hamilton, Dr. Robert "Bud" Littlefield, and Dr. Sally Stabb. Their service on my (PK) committee and their valuable advice were instrumental throughout my dissertation research.

I'd (JR) like to recognize Dr. Tom Smith, who encouraged me to sit down and write what I believe, and then always questioned those beliefs, thus making my thoughts stronger and full of depth.

I'd (PK) also like to recognize two very special women, my professional mentors, Dr. Delane Kinney and Ann Reese. I thank them for teaching me that the person of the therapist and the professional of the therapist are equally important and are not mutually exclusive. Their love, support, and encouragement over the years helped me to recognize the gifts that I've been given. They truly are treasures to our field, but I'm blessed to say treasures in my life.

We'd also like to thank Dr. Rudy Buckman and Dr. Phil Torti. They challenged us to think in many interesting ways. Our discussions, conversations, debates, jokes, and disagreements helped us to know that dialogues of true disagreement can be had without the presence of anger and negative feelings. We're thankful our paths crossed.

We'd like to recognize professionals such as Melissa Elliott who helped to pave the way for a work like ours. We're thankful for the friendships we've experienced with Dr. Carmen Cruz, Dr. Denise Lucero-Miller, Dr. Don Rosen, Dr. Gail Chester, Dr. Susan Mecca, Dr. Deborah Boelter, and Dr. Ron Garber.

Thanks also go out to Dr. Frank Thomas. He helped us to see that our shared experiences as class clowns in our youth could actually be a professional competency. His work in integrating humor and psychotherapy helped us to gain the courage to attempt some humor in this book while overcoming our fear that we'd end up seeing more birds than Ruben Kincaid on a multicolored tour bus.

Thanks go to my (PK) two best friends from my graduate training, Dr. Michael Johnson and Dr. Bonnie Osmon. Our shared faith and experiences truly made our graduate training more fulfilling and enjoyable.

Thanks also go to lifelong friends Mark Minick and Brian Smith. They helped support me (PK) through graduate training and still love me enough to pretend they have any interest in anything I might have to say about this project.

To our clients who helped us to see that avoidance of spiritual issues in therapy based on a fear of imposing one's own values is also a value imposition.

To all those who are brave enough to find learning in this book.

Finally, we pray that all readers and their families will be blessed with a growing sense of God's presence and power in their lives. May God's truth and justice guard their minds, may God's grace and mercy guard their hearts, and may God's peace, which transcends all understanding, guard their hearts and minds in the way of truth and love in life.

Power always brings with it responsibility. You cannot have power to work well without having so much power as to be able to work ill.

Theodore Roosevelt,
speech in Milwaukee,
September 7, 1910

Introduction to a Journey

THERAPIST: What has helped you make the healthy changes you've made in your life over the past year?

CLIENT: Including my faith in my therapeutic work! God was never a part of my treatment in the past. I was never able to gain a new perspective. Treatment seemed to focus on blaming things on my childhood; never about what I needed to do to get better. For me, past treatment, that included Prozac and psychoanalysis, didn't work. But this therapeutic work is very different and I'm seeing real therapeutic gains.

This is a brief excerpt from a session with a client who struggled for years with depression, bulimia, and relationship difficulties. Some professionals might be surprised to hear such comments during therapy. However, we often hear these types of comments in response to our open-ended questions during the course of therapy.

Some might argue, "You're imposing your values onto the client," "You're acting unethically by talking about God in therapy," or "Yes, but you two (Peter and John) are religious counselors. I don't consider myself a religious counselor, so I don't have those types of conversations during therapy." Quite honestly, we don't consider ourselves to be religious counselors either. We simply view ourselves as ethical counselors who work hard at helping our clients make positive life changes consistent with their reported values and spiritual and/or religious orientations. At the same time, we are very aware that many counselors find it easier to avoid these types of conversations than to enter into them. We understand this, because at one time we did the same.

Throughout this book, we'll share personal and professional stories related to our own "learned avoidance," and how we overcame it. We won't limit this discussion to our own experiences and theories, however. We'll consider historical perspectives on the suitability of integrating spirituality and psychotherapy and take on the challenge of presenting findings from numerous empirical studies without in-

sleep. Toward this goal, we'll integrate research find-
g those from our own study, and debunk the notion that
f religion, spirituality, and the history of psychotherapy
humor-free approach. Comic illustrations and other
or are used to invite you to consider these serious topics in unique ways for two important reasons. First, we don't believe humor causes any harm if it's used appropriately. We agree with C. S. Lewis, who said, "A little comic relief in a discussion does no harm, however serious the topic may be" (1958, p. 90). Second, we believe humor can be a powerful source of help for people throughout life's journey. Lewis also said, "Humor involves a sense of proportion and a power of seeing yourself from the outside" ([1961] 1996, p. 7).

One of the challenges encountered in an endeavor such as this is to differentiate between spirituality and religion. In so doing, it would be easy to give the impression that we see these terms as mutually exclusive. However, we don't. Although we acknowledge that some individuals consider these terms to be mutually exclusive, we are also aware that others see them as interrelated. We identify with the latter group, believing that spirituality and religion are neither mutually exclusive nor synonymous, but interrelated.

We have attended workshops on integrating spirituality and therapy in which the presenters didn't have the opportunity to fully address the information they'd planned to cover because some in the audience got into debates about how these terms should be defined. We thank one of our colleagues, Robert "Bud" Littlefield, for the use of one of his catch phrases with regard to these debates: "What that's about, isn't what that's about." Rather than attempt to do the impossible and come up with definitions with which everyone would agree, we simply offer the reader our definitions, revised from those of others.

> Spirituality refers to the uniquely personal and subjective experience of a fourth dimension; religion refers to the specific and concrete expression of spirituality. (Anderson and Worthen, 1997, p. 4)

The revision we suggest and assume in this book is as follows:

> Spirituality refers to the uniquely personal and subjective experience of God; religion refers to the specific and concrete expression of spirituality.

Some may see this revision as a minor change, and others will see a major one. Some may agree with our definitions, and others may disagree. We welcome such disagreement, for we hold no illusory belief that our attempts to define spirituality and religion will encompass the belief systems of everyone. In fact, this is the very reason we made this change. Why? First, this change better represents our own belief systems. Second, we suggest that anyone who would propose that there are all-inclusive definitions that encompass all spiritual and religious traditions is simply demonstrating a need for further self-examination of his or her own beliefs. Why? (Appropriate use of silence here may help the reader move toward his or her own answers to this question. If not, stay tuned.)

In Section I, "Jousting with the Pink Elephants," we explore some of the factors that contribute to the current state of training in the mental health care fields related to the integration of religion, spirituality, and psychotherapy. The pink elephant analogy is a familiar one to those who work in counseling-related fields. For example, a family that includes an alcoholic parent may have a pink elephant in the middle of its living room if the family members ignore the alcoholism and/or pretend it's not really a problem. Some family members may be aware of the alcoholism but choose to ignore the problem for fear that the alcoholic parent's denial may lead to further pain, perhaps even an unpleasant confrontation. It's important to note that this phenomenon isn't the exclusive property of families in which alcohol is abused. A professional family can also have a pink elephant in the middle of its profession, choosing to ignore the problem, perhaps out of fear of possible negative consequences. In this section, we look at some of the pink elephants that have been living in the center of the family home of the mental health care fields for many years now. We also explore how this "learned avoidance" has impacted therapists' willingness and ability to engage in God talk in therapy.

In Section II, "How Then Shall We Counsel?", we move beyond the pink elephants to explore some of the factors that can help therapists become more competent clinicians with regard to integrating spirituality and psychotherapy. Nothing in our field is safe as we address the integration of the sacred in the field of psychotherapy. Topics such as truth, belief, postmodernism, open-mindedness, all-inclusiveness, and many more powerful issues don't go unexamined as we explore how therapists can learn to stand (and of course sit) in reverence of power. For indeed, spirituality can be both a powerfully helpful, and hurtful, source of influence in therapy.

So without further ado, we invite the reader to join us in a process of exploration and self-examination. We hope that readers will experience this book as a journey of self-discovery rather than as a task they engage in to be educated by others. As Galileo once said, "You cannot teach a man anything; you can only help him find it for himself." This, indeed, is our hope for our readers. However, we would offer a slight modification for therapists of the twenty-first century: "You cannot teach individuals anything; you can only help them find it for themselves." With this in mind, enjoy the journey!

Note to the reader: Although we use gender-neutral language throughout this book, we've chosen to leave the quotations cited in this work as they were originally written to respect the historical accuracy of the authors' words. Also, to protect the confidentiality of the clients, supervisees, and co-workers mentioned throughout, the names of these individuals (in some cases even their gender), and in some other cases even the actual therapist involved, were altered to ensure that these individuals are unidentifiable.

SECTION I: JOUSTING WITH THE PINK ELEPHANTS

Elephants endors'd with towers.

John Milton

Chapter 1

Walking on Silent Eggshells

Religious liberty might be supposed to mean that everybody is free to discuss religion. In practice it means that hardly anybody is allowed to mention it.

G. K. Chesterton
Autobiography

THE FEAR OF AUTHENTICITY

"Peter, how are you, as a Christian, going to keep your values out of therapy when you're working with clients who aren't Christians?" I can hear those words ring in my ears as though they had been spoken yesterday. There I was, a twenty-six-year-old graduate student, sitting in my practicum training class, being asked the same question that I had been asked on at least three prior occasions. In each of those past instances, the inquisitor had been one of my professors. On this day, however, the question was coming from one of my fellow students. Before I responded, I paused and took a deep breath. I was aware that my thoughts were going in a number of different directions. How should I respond? How does she know that I'm a Christian? Do I trust the people in the room? What's the politically correct response to this question? How honest and open can I be? How honest and open *should* I be? As I considered how to respond, something within me led me to think, You've answered this question a number of times before. This time, however, don't feel as if you're being challenged. Instead, use this as an opportunity to challenge. The voice within me was somewhat different from the one I had experienced in the past. Rather than being inauthentic and acting from a position of fear, I felt a peaceful confidence come over me as I smiled and replied: "That's a great question and one that definitely needs to be examined. However, I find myself wondering today why I've had this question posed to me numerous times in the past, and yet not once have I heard the alternative question posed to my atheistic and agnostic friends. So, let me simply ask you a question: How are you, as a non-Christian, going to keep your values out of therapy, when you're working with clients who are Christians?" One could have heard a pin drop as silence came over the room. My classmate appeared to be stunned by my response. In my peripheral vision, I noticed some movement from where my professor was sitting. I glanced at her and noticed that she was smiling as she looked intently at my stunned classmate, apparently eager to hear her response.

What ensued was the first productive discussion in which I had ever participated in a graduate class regarding the fact that every therapist has personal values of which he or she needs to be aware, before, during, and after therapy sessions. It was also the first time I ever felt free to talk about spiritual beliefs in a classroom setting. This interchange led me to wonder, Why? Why had I been afraid to tell people at my graduate school that I'm a Christian? Where did I get the idea that I would be committing professional suicide if I talked about spiritual issues in regard to therapy? Where did I get the notion that I would be out of line for simply posing logical questions to others about their own spiritual assumptions and beliefs as they relate to therapy? Where did I get the idea that it was unethical to discuss spirituality in therapy? In fact, where did I learn to avoid initiating *any* discussion of spirituality in graduate training? These questions, in turn, led to more questions. I began a process of deep exploration and self-examination, because I wanted to learn more about why I had learned to avoid discussions of spirituality in professional settings.

SELF-REFLEXIVITY

We believe that self-reflexivity is one of the most important responsibilities of the competent therapist. We also believe it is a process often neglected. Even when self-reflexivity is attempted, it is often done halfheartedly or half-honestly. We've encouraged all of our trainees and supervisees to develop the habit of exploring the influence that their own personal beliefs, assumptions, and biases can have on the therapeutic process. These self-reflexive habits (Griffith and Griffith, 1992) are employed to help practitioners increase their awareness of how their own beliefs influence the types of questions they ask, which topics they are more likely to attend to as their clients share their stories, which topics they tend to marginalize and/or minimize as those stories are shared, and the degree to which they do or do not like and/or respect their clients.

We believe that self-reflexivity is not an event, but rather is a continual process of self-examination that all therapists need to employ throughout therapy with every client. Self-reflexive habits are based on the premise that the therapist's awareness will increase, and that this increased awareness will help to decrease the influence of the therapist's biases which could be hurtful to the therapeutic process. It's also possible that self-reflexivity can help to increase the influence of the therapist's healthy beliefs, those which could be helpful to the therapeutic process. Toward this goal, practitioners who are religious are encouraged to examine how their beliefs may impact the therapeutic process, either positively or negatively. Similarly, practitioners who are not religious are also encouraged to examine how their beliefs may impact the therapeutic process, either positively or negatively. In summary, self-reflexivity is a process designed to make the covert overt by helping therapists increase their awareness of the influence that their subconscious can have on the therapeutic process.

Self-Reflexercise

We now invite you to join us in a self-reflexive exercise. Imagine that you are awaiting the arrival of a new client with whom you have never had contact. Imagine that the individual had arranged the appointment through your intake receptionist, providing very little information. In fact, the only information you received, other than the appointment date and time, was a statement made by the client and recorded by the receptionist during their brief phone conversation. Five minutes remain before the scheduled appointment time. Your receptionist hands you the new client's file with the brief information already mentioned, including the following statement:

> Jesus is eternally right. History is replete with the bleached bones of nations that refused to listen to him. May we in the twentieth century hear and follow his words—before it is too late.

Now, we invite you to consider some questions. After each question, we encourage you to pause for open and honest reflection.

- Do you agree with the client's statement on the intake form? If so, why? If not, why?
- If you agree with this statement, do you think it would be easier for you to work with this client than if you didn't agree with the statement? If so, why? If not, why?
- If you don't agree with the statement, do you think it would be more of a challenge for you to work with this client? If so, why? If not, why?
- Are you aware of any internal reaction to this statement?
- Do you think that reading this statement will influence you in any way during the first session?
- Has it already influenced your evaluation of the client before your first meeting? If so, why? If not, why?
- Do you think it would be a challenge for you to work with this client? If so, why? If not, why?
- Have you mentally attached a gender to this person?
- Do you believe that the client's statement is demonstrative of a person who is narrow-minded or open-minded?

We encourage you to take some time to be aware of and reflect upon your internal conversations, or self-talk, related to this exercise.

Now, imagine starting over with the same scenario, except that this time you have one new piece of information about the client. One minute before the scheduled appointment, your receptionist hands you a revised intake form. It's exactly the same as the previous sheet, with one exception. The new sheet reads as follows:

> Jesus is eternally right. History is replete with the bleached bones of nations that refused to listen to him. May we in the twentieth century hear and follow his words—before it is too late.
>
> Dr. Jerry Falwell

- Did anything within you just change? If so, why? If not, why?
- Did your initial intake plans just change? If so, why? If not, why?

- Would you welcome this opportunity to have Dr. Jerry Falwell as your new client? If so, why? If not, why?
- Would working with this client be more of a challenge, now that you know who the client is?

How do your responses to these questions inform you about who you are as the person of the therapist?

UNPACKING LEARNED AVOIDANCE

The exploration for answers regarding why I had learned to avoid discussing spirituality in professional settings, beginning with my experience in the practicum class, led me to reflect on a number of different sources of influence. First of all, it was helpful to look within myself at the internal factors. No one had held a gun to my head, ordering me to avoid such discussions. Yet something within me strongly believed that I would be doing something wrong and/or unethical if I were to talk about spirituality with my clients. This belief influenced my behavior not only in therapy sessions but also in training contexts. I had definitely avoided conversations of spirituality, because of my belief that talking about spirituality in psychological contexts was somehow "against the rules." Rather than stopping my self-examination at this point, I delved further into this belief in an attempt to discover where I had received messages that supported this notion.

It's likely that societal messages played a formative role in the process of acquiring learned avoidance. The old adage "Whatever you do, don't talk about religion or politics" sends a very clear message. If you want to avoid awkwardness and/or discomfort, you'd be wise to avoid discussing these issues.

Strong messages were also received from peers about the risks of discussing issues of spirituality in professional settings. I recall that during the first semester of my graduate training I had a conversation with a fellow classmate who I had just discovered was also a Christian. After class one day, we were talking about some of the things we had just heard in our philosophy class. As we walked along, our discussion turned toward the challenge of being Christians and in training to be therapists. My new friend stopped and said, "Whatever you do, make sure that you don't talk about your faith here." "Hold on,"

I responded, "that goes against the very fabric of what psychology is about . . . being authentic and open about who we are as human beings." He smiled and said, "I love your idealism, but if you're authentic about your faith, you'll risk not making it through the program. One day you'll come to understand that Christian beliefs aren't always compatible with the dominant beliefs in our society and in our program." I responded, "I understand that completely, but that doesn't necessarily mean that I have to keep my faith a secret." He replied, "I had the same struggle when I first arrived here. So, I talked with a friend of mine who is a minister. He asked me a great question: 'Can you be more influential for God with a PhD or without a PhD? If the answer is with a PhD, then simply keep your mouth shut and do whatever it takes to get through the program. There will be plenty of time to speak up for God after you get your degree.'" I'll never forget that interchange. I remember parting ways with him that day and walking away thinking, "Wow, what a dim view of life as a grad student." Even though I didn't necessarily enjoy hearing what he said, I have no doubt that our conversation helped shape my views about the risks associated with discussing one's spiritual beliefs in graduate training.

A year or so later, I was sitting in a room with about six other practicum students and two supervisors listening to one of my colleagues give a formalized case presentation. After watching a video clip from a session in which the client had talked briefly about her spiritual beliefs as they related to the life issues with which she was dealing, we began to exchange ideas about the case. One practicum therapist asked the presenter, "Have you considered the real possibility that your client has a thought disorder?" The presenter responded, "No, I haven't, but tell me what you heard that makes you think she might have a thought disorder." "Well," came the reply, "your client made the comment that although she was down about her current situation, she had faith that God was going to take care of her no matter what happens to her in life. That type of belief is often indicative of individuals with low self-esteem who can't take responsibility for themselves." I remember thinking, "There's an antispiritual bias if I ever heard one," and yet her assertion was actually supported by another therapist in training. They agreed that perhaps the therapist should challenge the client related to this type of thinking. I found it difficult to believe what I was hearing. After further discussion on this idea, one of the supervisors finally spoke up and made the point that the client's statement could also be demonstrative of an individual who simply has a deep, personal faith in God. I was glad that the supervisor had spoken up, and yet I remember leaving that case presentation feeling drained and perplexed, wondering, Should I have said something? If I had said something, would people have questioned my self-esteem, mental health, maturity, and/or intelligence? Would they have believed that perhaps I, too, had a thought disorder?

Throughout my graduate training, I heard many other things that made me question whether I should talk about spirituality and religion at all. The antireligious and aspiritualistic biases in graduate school were not limited to clinical training settings. These biases were alive and thriving in the classroom and other didactic training environments, nurtured by professionals in positions of power and authority. Whether it was a professor who said, "Saint Augustine's biggest mistake was his position that faith in God is more important than human reason," or a clinical trainer who said, "Nietzsche was correct. God is dead," or a clinical supervisor, who, in response to a question addressing individuals who don't have a spiritual orientation, said, "Perhaps they're simply smart enough to think on their own," the messages I received were very clear. Some professionals in the mental health fields believe, "To believe in God, is to demonstrate a weakness, an unhealthy dependency, and/or a cognitive deficit."

My own professional experiences led me to discuss this subject with John, who was one of my supervisors at that time. Many of my clients were talking about how important God was in their lives, yet I didn't know what to do when they would make such comments. John shared with me stories of challenges he had faced as a Christian in various professional settings.

Although I (JR) could identify with some of the things that Peter shared with me, my personal experiences in training and supervision took on a somewhat different form. As I discovered, sometimes in avoiding the subject, a clear message is sent to trainees to not talk about the subject. I sat in classes in which I heard lectures and participated in discussions regarding gender, race, ethnicity, SES (socioeconomic status), sexual orientation, and most every other issue that therapists work with in therapy. I also took classes on special issues and special populations. I assure you, my training was thorough. Yet there was never a discussion of spirituality in general, let alone a discussion of the integration of spirituality in therapy. I found this interesting in light of the fact that this topic seemed to be quite pervasive in the lives of the families with whom I was working as a practicum therapist. Although I was not aware of it at the time, the absence of any discussions of spirituality in graduate school sent a loud, clear message to not talk about it at all. The messages I received during my training and supervision experiences were more covert in nature than were the messages Peter received in his training, but interestingly enough the net effect was the same. Indeed, this was the type of silence that speaks!

These shared experiences led us to wonder whether other psychotherapists had received similar messages about the integration of spirituality and psychotherapy, and whether such messages had influenced them to avoid discussions of spirituality in professional settings. Indeed, our journey was just beginning.

Chapter 2

Sources of Influence

Religion is the most important social force in the history of man. . . . But in psychology, anyone who gets involved in or tries to talk in an analytic, careful way about religion is immediately branded a meathead; a mystic; an intuitive, touchy-feely sort of moron.

Robert Hogan
in *APA Monitor*

MAPPING THE INFLUENCE OF LEARNED AVOIDANCE

Robert Hogan, a section editor for the *Journal of Personality and Social Psychology,* made this statement in 1979. Some eighteen years later, after coming to a similar conclusion based on our experiences, John and I started work on the research study that served as the integral part of my dissertation. During my proposal defense, one of the professors who served on my dissertation committee asked, "Peter, what type of return rate do you expect to get?" I responded, "Based on the history of the research approach I'm using, I expect to get approximately forty percent of the packets completed and returned." She smiled and wished me good luck, adding, "Based on past research, you'll be lucky to get thirty-three percent back."

In 1997, we mailed 300 survey packets to licensed practitioners in the state of Texas, 150 to licensed psychologists and 150 to licensed marriage and family therapists who were randomly selected from their respected Texas state rosters. Eleven of the packets were returned as undeliverable. Of the remaining 289 potential participants, 155 surveys were returned, yielding *a return rate of 53.6 percent.* However, four of the returned surveys were not utilized in the final sample because the respondents did not provide responses to the questions in two of the sections on the questionnaire. Therefore, the final sample consisted of 151 licensed practitioners in the state of Texas, including 83 women and 67 men (one participant did not indicate gender), and 76 psychologists and 75 marriage and family therapists. Obviously, the return rate far exceeded my expectations and the expectations of my professor.

In addition to getting some useful quantitative data from the survey, we posed six open-ended questions to the participants in an attempt to get useful qualitative information as well. The written responses to the six open-ended questions were analyzed and reviewed for content-based themes. The responses to each question were divided into groups based on preliminary themes. These themes were then analyzed to determine the number of responses contained within each specific grouping of comments. In this study, similar responses were classified as a theme if at least 10 percent ($n = 15$) of the total sample contributed a response to the particular theme. Finally, the themes were analyzed again to determine the frequencies and proportions of psychologists and marriage and family therapists who contributed a comment to each theme.

The overwhelming majority of respondents provided written responses to the open-ended questions. A number of the participants' responses were extensive and lengthy. In fact, some of the participants included additional pages of comments in response to the questions posed. When one considers the return rate (53.6 percent), and the fact that many of these participants included additional handwritten comments with their returned surveys, it seems safe to conclude that the discussion of spirituality in therapy engenders a great deal of energy within the mental health field.

The responses to the qualitative question "Where have you received messages that discouraged discussion of God in therapy?" proved to be very informative (see Table 2.1). Not surprisingly, the theme containing the largest number of respondents was "graduate school/training." Interestingly, the theme containing the second largest number of respondents was "training (other or unspecified)." Eleven of the respondents indicated receiving messages in both "graduate school/training" and "training (other or unspecified)" that discouraged discussion of God in therapy. Due to this finding, one can't simply add 33.8 percent and 21.2 percent together to get the total percentage of respondents who indicated they had received messages in

TABLE 2.1. Responses to "Where have you received messages that discouraged discussion of God in therapy?"

Theme	LMFT ($n = 75$)	Psych. ($n = 76$)	Total ($n = 151$)
Graduate school/training	27 (36.0%)	24 (31.6%)	51 (33.8%)
Training (other or unspecified)	10 (13.3%)	22 (28.9%)	32 (21.2%)
Nowhere/did not receive such messages	13 (17.3%)	14 (18.4%)	27 (17.9%)
Self/personal approach to therapy	13 (17.3%)	14 (18.4%)	27 (17.9%)
Colleagues/peers	5 (6.7%)	11 (14.5%)	16 (10.6%)
Work site	11 (14.7%)	4 (5.3%)	15 (9.9%)

Note: LMFT = licensed marriage and family therapist; Psych. = licensed psychologist

some form of training that discouraged discussion of God in therapy. When this effect was taken into account, we discovered that sixty-nine (45.7 percent) of the respondents indicated that they received messages that discouraged discussion of God in therapy in some form of professional training. Our original question was answered; we learned that we were not the only ones who had received messages in graduate school and other forms of professional training that discouraged discussing spiritual issues in therapy. In fact, nearly half of the respondents indicated they had received such messages. (*Note:* These were open-ended questions. No response categories were imposed on the participants.)

We found some of the written responses to the questions quite interesting. The following is a sample of some of the responses we received. Indeed, sometimes it's more helpful to hear the words from the "horse's mouth," so to speak. (Accordingly, the responses remain unaltered from their original form.)

> *If you wish to know the mind of a man, listen to his words.*
>
> Chinese Proverb

Participants used some of the following comments to answer the open-ended question, "Where have you received messages that discouraged discussion of God in therapy?"

Graduate School/Training (33.8 Percent)

- "During graduate training."
- "Graduate school—'God is unscientific' . . ."
- "In general, discouragement came from academic professors & supervisors whether this was intentional or not the idea was conveyed that discussion of God or religion was a Taboo subject."
- "Graduate school—Told that discussing God was unethical in that my opinions may push the client to believe as I do."

Training—Other or Unspecified (21.2 Percent)

- "Formal training, Go to a minister for spirituality, go to a therapist for therapy."
- "Post grad training."
- "I believe that the message that religion doesn't belong there is more in the omission of it in training."
- "University setting, Ethics workshops."
- "In every aspect of my training."

Nowhere/Did Not Receive Such Messages (17.9 Percent)

- "I don't recall ever being actively discouraged from doing so."
- "No where—(or else, I thought the message too silly to take seriously)."
- "I haven't."
- "Although I am aware that there are those messages, I disagree—c.e. I did not 'receive' or accept those messages."

Self/Personal Approach to Therapy (17.9 Percent)

- "Self—Do not impose my religious views on others."
- "Common Sense."
- "I strongly believe the idea of turning problems over to 'God' disempowers people and also may be an abnegator of responsibility in dealing with life's problems."
- "I personally think that it is a personal decision. If client brings it up, fine but I will not bring it up."

Colleagues/Peers (10.6 Percent)

- "Peer attitudes."
- "From colleagues in the universities."
- "Other professionals."
- "Never—wait. Once a colleague I respected disparaged religious beliefs."

Work Site (9.9 Percent)

- "When employed by the state hospital it was strongly discouraged."
- "Public funded agency."
- "During my employment in public mental health."
- "In every agency I have worked in, both private and public it has been actively discouraged."

We're sure you'll agree that these findings reveal some very interesting information. A picture starts to form that provides insight into some of the causes of learned avoidance. However, these findings take on even greater significance in light of the findings associated with the responses to another one of the open-ended questions in the study. In an attempt to gain more insight into potential sources of influence, we asked the participants the same question, with the exception of replacing the word *discouraged* with the word *encouraged.* Responses to the question, "Where have you received messages that encouraged discussion of God in therapy?" are shown in Table 2.2.

Again, we believe it's important to see the words of these psychologists and marriage and family therapists to gain an even richer, deeper understanding of their experiences as they relate to the open-ended question, "Where have you received messages that encouraged discussion of God in therapy?"

> *A word is dead when it is said, some say. I say it just begins to live that day.*
>
> Emily Dickinson
> "A Word Is Dead"

TABLE 2.2. Responses to "Where have you received messages that encouraged discussion of God in therapy?"

Theme	LMFT ($n = 75$)	Psych. ($n = 76$)	Total ($n = 151$)
Patients/clients	24 (32.0%)	22 (28.9%)	46 (30.5%)
Religious counselors or professionals	17 (22.7%)	10 (13.2%)	27 (17.9%)
Colleagues/peers	13 (17.3%)	12 (15.8%)	25 (16.6%)
Personal religious/spiritual beliefs and/or experiences	19 (25.3%)	6 (7.9%)	25 (16.6%)
Specific presenting issues/problems	12 (16.0%)	13 (17.1%)	25 (16.6%)
Nowhere/did not receive such messages	6 (8.0%)	14 (18.4%)	20 (13.2%)
Training (other or unspecified)	5 (6.6%)	10 (13.2%)	15 (9.9%)

Note: LMFT = licensed marriage and family therapist; Psych. = licensed psychologist

Patients/Clients (30.5 Percent)

- "Also, yes from Jewish patients."
- "Many of the clients ask for and encourage spiritual discussion."
- "Constantly from clients in serious conflict or in great need of spiritual support."
- "The encouragement has been from client interest."
- "When clients bring up God; clients who are not angry if God is brought up."

Religious Counselors or Professionals (17.9 Percent)

- "Seminars, usually those of a religious nature. Example, National Conference for Christian Counselors."
- "Pastoral counselors."
- "American Association of Christian Counselors—a group of Christian graduate students I organized to meet weekly for a brown-bag lunch to discuss our training in light of Christian principles."
- "I honestly cannot think of any source other than discussion with hospital chaplains."

Colleagues/Peers (16.6 Percent)

- "Peer attitudes."
- "Other therapists."
- "Nowhere, except for very few colleagues who understand/accept/believe in importance of one's spiritual world view in mental health."

Personal Religious/Spiritual Beliefs and/or Experiences (16.6 Percent)

Interestingly, 25.3 percent of LMFTs made comments that fell under this theme, and only 7.9 percent of the psychologists made comments that fell under this theme.

- "In my experience helping others I have found that if spirituality, whether or not God is named is not part of treatment no lasting change is as likely as if spirituality is allowed and made a part of change."
- "Mainly in my personal pursuits for spiritual growth."
- "My own beliefs about the value of being religious and spiritual."
- "From my own convictions which are based on the teachings of the Holy Bible."
- "My own views and desire of clients to do so."

Specific Presenting Issues/Problems (16.6 Percent)

- "From my work in the alcohol and drug field. AA is an important resource for many people in recovery and from AA they learn to address their spirituality as part of recovery."
- "Also in my work dealing with cancer patients and others dealing with terminal illness."
- "Primarily from years working with persons in acute situations."
- "Patients esp. older, disabled, ill pts."
- "I don't need 'messages' to discuss basic issues of life and death, pain, suffering, joy, solace."

Nowhere/Did Not Receive Such Messages (13.2 Percent)

- "No where."
- "I haven't."
- "I have not received messages that encourage discussion of God in therapy."
- "I don't know that I have received messages any type of info that would encourage religion in therapy."

Training (Other or Unspecified) (9.9 Percent)

- "My training emphasized the spiritual aspect of therapy significantly."
- "My training made me open to human concerns and needs—God and spirituality are very important to many of my clients."
- "I have attended workshops and read books and articles (Larry Dossey) about these aspects which have helped me rethink my views."
- "Seminars, usually those of a religious nature."
- "My clinical mentor is a strong advocate of psycho-spiritual therapy."

THE ONGOING INFLUENCE OF MIXED MESSAGES

Based on these findings, although clients and/or patients often give therapists messages indicating they would like to talk about God in therapy, many of these therapists are forced to confront the messages they received during training that discouraged them from having such discussions in therapy. It seems that many therapists have received more mixed signals than a batter getting signs from an indecisive third-base coach standing in poison ivy. For the competent therapist, this raises important questions. Whom will I serve? If I respect a client's desire to discuss his or her spiritual faith in therapy, how then shall I counsel?

These are extremely important questions to entertain because therapists' assumptions and beliefs can and do influence their behavior in how they approach spiritual issues in therapy. It's quite clear that many therapists have beliefs that undoubtedly impact how they address spiritual issues in therapy. Some of the research participants apparently believed such concepts as "To discuss God in therapy is to be unethical," "Because there is a risk of imposing your values onto the client, it is best to not talk about God in therapy," and "Spirituality and therapy are mutually exclusive." Sometimes having assumptions and/or beliefs such as these can unfortunately lead therapists to believe that they have professional freedom to avoid discussions of spirituality in therapy. However, rather than simply assuming that these sources of influence do, indeed, influence the practice of therapists when confronted with spiritual issues in therapy, we decided to examine this theory further.

Chapter 3

The Influence of the Person of the Therapist

We can easily forgive a child who is afraid of the dark; the real tragedy of life is when men are afraid of the light.

Plato

EARLY INFLUENCE

We both had schoolteachers who taught us early on about the potential dangers of assumptions and jumping to conclusions. I (PK) remember my physical science teacher in ninth grade addressing this subject in class one day after several students had made the same mistake because they had misunderstood a question our teacher had posed on a test, but had failed to ask him for further clarification. He wrote the word "assume" on the board and then posed a question to our class. He asked, "Does anyone know what the definition of this word is?" He went on to say, "The definition of the word assume resides within the word itself." Then, he wrote the word on the board again, but this time he added two spaces, so the word read as follows:

ASS U ME

He then said, "You better base the decisions you make in life on something more than assumptions. For if you make decisons like you did on this test, making assumptions without asking questions for further clarification, you'll end up making an ass out of you and me."

Similarly, I (JR) was in a Western Civilization class when the teacher was discussing a famous military general who had made some quick decisions, based on false assumptions about how to approach a certain battle, that contributed to the general and his troops losing the battle. I'll never forget how he finished the lesson. He said, "Listen kids, jumping to conclusions is like jumping into the shower. I can guarantee that eventually you will slip and fall." You just don't get these types of quality educational experiences in private schools. Be that as it may, they are definitely learning experiences we won't soon forget about the dangers of making assumptions and jumping to conclusions without seeking more information for further clarification.

SOME CONSTRAINTS AND RESTRAINTS TO INTEGRATION

Melissa Elliott (Griffith, 1995b) suggests that sometimes both clients and therapists are responsible for limiting or avoiding God talk in therapy, even though this conversation could be quite helpful. She proposes that some therapists, as well as some clients, want to talk about religious issues in therapy if they can be helpful to the client. Thus, she poses the question: "Given that therapists, counselors, and clients want these conversations to occur, what underlying assumptions lead us, unaware, to constrain them?" (p. 125).

Lovinger (1979) suggests that a therapist may omit religion from therapy because of strong personal feelings toward religion (both negative and positive), a simplistic view of religious experience, and/or fears that the therapist may include his or her values in therapy. Since personal and professional issues may influence a therapist's willingness to address religious issues during the course of therapy, it seems reasonable to suggest that he or she should explore the influence these biases may have on his or her clinical practice (Miller, 1992).

Based on responses from an interdisciplinary group of therapists attending a seminar, James Griffith and Melissa Elliott (Griffith and Griffith, 1997) compiled an inventory of constraints that had, in the past, obstructed therapists from entering into therapeutic conversations involving religious issues. The therapists reported the following factors had restricted them from entering into such therapeutic conversations: professional injunctions, interpersonal monologues, lack of common culture, views that religion limits gender roles, remembered cultural admonitions, societal discourse (e.g., religion and politics), views that religious conversations are not practical for therapy, and uncertainty/fear about how one should handle self-disclosure. These therapists also reported that certain things, such as a safe setting, academic freedom, clarity about one's personal sense of spirituality, and the development of a collaborative relationship, helped encourage them to enter into conversations involving religious issues with their clients. Therefore, these therapists acknowledged that personal and professional issues had influenced them in the past, acting as either constraints that limited conversations involving religious issues or progressive pathways that opened space for spiritual conversations to take place.

Based on the responses of the participants in this seminar and our respect for the work of James Griffith and Melissa Elliott, we decided to address these issues in greater depth in an empirical manner. To avoid hypothesizing about whether certain messages actually influenced therapists in therapy, we simply posed a question that asked the therapists to report the beliefs and/or assumptions they hold that have discouraged them from talking about spiritual issues in therapy. The responses to the question "What assumptions and/or beliefs do you have that discouraged you to talk about God in therapy?" provided some important information (see Table 3.1).

Many therapists reported that they have assumptions and/or beliefs that, in fact, had discouraged them from talking about God in therapy. Again, we believe that the therapists' own words provide greater insight into these assumptions and/or beliefs.

A Discussion in Therapy About Spirituality Is Not Helpful, Harmful, and/or Inappropriate (21.2 Percent)

- "Need to separate spirituality from therapy."
- "Separation of Church and State."
- "Only the possibility of doing harm rather than helping."
- "That in some pts it is counterproductive to reinforce religious pre-occupation."
- "With some clients this area could be one which creates a barrier between therapist client, e.g., a devout atheist, agnostic, etc."

TABLE 3.1. Responses to "What assumptions and/or beliefs do you have that discouraged you to talk about God in therapy?"

Theme	LMFT (*n* = 75)	Psych. (*n* = 76)	Total (*n* = 151)
A discussion in therapy about spirituality is not helpful, harmful, and/or inappropriate	15 (20.0%)	17 (22.4%)	32 (21.2%)
Concern about imposing own values onto the client	11 (14.6%)	13 (17.1%)	24 (15.9%)
Client must initiate any conversation regarding spirituality/religion	16 (21.3%)	6 (7.9%)	22 (14.6%)
None	11 (14.6%)	9 (11.8%)	20 (13.2%)
Client is not open/does not want to discuss spirituality in therapy	11 (14.6%)	7 (9.2%)	18 (11.9%)
Fear of being percieved as judging, preaching, or proselytizing	5 (6.6%)	10 (13.2%)	15 (9.9%)

Note: LMFT = licensed marriage and family therapist; Psych. = licensed psychologist

Concern About Imposing Own Values onto the Client (15.9 Percent)

- "I can't impose my belief system on anyone else."
- "I do not want to project my own issues onto the client."
- "I would never attempt to impose my concepts or beliefs about God or religion on my clients."
- "I had concern that my own beliefs about God would prejudice my ability to be an objective and careful listener."
- "I do not impress/interject my religion or spiritual beliefs on a client."

Client Must Initiate Any Conversation Regarding Spirituality/Religion (14.6 Percent)

- "Theology only should be used when it is part of the client's strengths and initiated by the client."
- "Hence, if I do not hear that religion or God is an issue for the client, I don't bring up the issue."

- "My feeling is that the therapist probably should not be the one to initiate conversation on this topic, unless perhaps the client first manifests problems/concerns related to religion."
- "I do not believe that God has a place in therapy, and can't under any circumstances imagine bringing up God in a therapy session unless the client is discussing the subject."

None (13.2 Percent)

- "None—I refuse to work with clients who do not accept this perspective."
- "At the present, none. Formerly, I was taught to view psychotherapy as a scientist and to take a rational, objective stance."
- "I do not have any."

Client Is Not Open/Does Not Want to Discuss Spirituality in Therapy (11.9 Percent)

- "Some people who are clients do not wish to discuss these issues. It is therefore important to accept their personal boundaries."
- "Client doesn't want to."
- "Only if the client/clients are uncomfortable or unresponsive."
- "May turn some people off—That is not where the client wants to go."
- "That if a person does not respond to a casual introduction of faith/God as a topic I would desist."

Fear of Being Perceived As Judging, Preaching, or Proselytizing (9.9 Percent)

- "Fear of being perceived as 'preaching'. My task is to comfort the wounded, not convert them."
- "I was very cautious about being perceived as proselytizing or pushing my beliefs."
- "The alcoholic or drug addict who is presently using and very defensive who feel even more guilt if they felt they were being preached to."
- "I find proslytizing (sp?) offensive."

This information clearly lends support to the finding that some therapists readily acknowledge that their beliefs and assumptions influence their openness to discuss spiritual issues in therapy. Of course, part of our work as therapists is to question and explore the beliefs and assumptions of our clients to make sure they are not falling into the trap of turning rationalized, false assumptions into unhealthy beliefs and practices. Therefore, it would seem wise to examine some of the beliefs and assumptions that are clearly evident in these findings. For brevity's sake, at this point, we simply examine two of the assumptions and/or beliefs that were overtly apparent in the previous comments. Other assumptions, beliefs, and "misbeliefs" that are prevalent today are addressed in later chapters.

SEPARATION OF CHURCH AND STATE

Some respondents suggested that the concept of separation of church and state had played a role in discouraging them from talking about God in therapy. We assume that the therapists who made these statements either worked in state agencies and/or in state universities. If not, the contention that this would be an issue would be a moot point, unless of course a therapist who works for a religious agency was assuming that he or she could not counsel state employees. Assuming this is not the case, and we hope this is a safe assumption, let's examine the question "Would talking about God in therapy, even in a state agency, constitute a violation of the laws related to the separation of church and state?"

Let's first address other assumptions that are present within the larger assumption. Is talking about God the equivalent of "church"? Perhaps this argument would have some merit if the client and the therapist, a state or government employee, were to take part in liturgy, sing hymns of praise, pray together, participate in sacraments, etc. However, does talking about one's faith and/or talking about God's comfort in one's life constitute a "church activity"? Personally, we don't think that it does. However, even if one believes that all discussions about God are necessarily "church activities," does that automatically mean that it's against the law to talk about one's spiritual faith in therapy? Let's examine this further by using an analogous illustration.

Is incest against the law? Yes. Would incest, if it occurred in the therapy room, be against the law? Yes. However, is it against the law to discuss issues related to incest in therapy? Of course it's not. In fact, therapists understand the reality that this tragic topic is addressed during the course of therapy with many clients.

Some will no doubt argue, "You two are way off. Incest and church are two completely different things." We certainly agree with that assertion. Indeed, incest and church are not even apples and oranges. However, the issue at hand is the quality and consistency of the logic, not the existence of synonyms. The assumption that simply discussing spiritual issues in therapy, even in a state agency, is against the law appears to be a leap of logic. Unfortunately, under examination, the logic appears to leap into illogic. This shouldn't surprise anyone since this type of leap into illogic has occurred in other areas of our society as well. Others, such as comedian Dennis Miller, have noticed this, too.

> Isn't it great we live in a country where a federal appeals court can declare the pledge of allegiance unconstitutional because the words "under God" are a violation of separation of church and state? Well, you know something, your honors, following that logic wouldn't the fact that you were sworn in with your hand on the Bible render you unemployed? Or maybe we should respond by withholding your obviously unconstitutional in-God-we-trust paycheck? Or why don't we just change the phrase to "one nation under a crushing blanket of overly sensitive political correctness"? (Miller, 2002)

Perhaps that ninth-grade physical science teacher had more depth than was originally thought. Regardless, the values of the person of the professional can, and do, influence one's beliefs about the ethicality and/or legality of a particular issue.

Another assumption and/or belief that was apparent in the responses of some of the therapists who participated in our study was that it was perhaps inappropriate or unethical to talk about spirituality in therapy. Indeed, this is a common assumption in our field that has reached the status of belief for many individuals and in many circles. Therefore, we believe that a more comprehensive examination is needed to appropriately address the question.

Chapter 4

To Be (Ethical) or Not to Be? What Is the Question?

A problem well-defined is half-solved.

Josh McDowell

THE ETHICS OF RELIGION IN THERAPY

There is a growing trend within the mental health community to view religion as a cultural factor that plays an important role in the lives of many individuals in the United States (Clay, 1996). For example, Section 1.1 of the *AAMFT Code of Ethics* (AAMFT, 2001) reads,

> Marriage and family therapists provide professional assistance to persons without discrimination on the basis of race, age, ethnicity, socioeconomic status, disability, gender, health status, *religion,* national origin, or sexual orientation. (p. 2)

Principle E in the Ethical Principles of Psychologists and Code of Conduct (APA, 2002) reads:

> Psychologists respect the dignity and worth of all people, and the rights of individuals to privacy, confidentiality, and self-determination. Psychologists are aware that special safeguards may be necessary to protect the rights and welfare of persons of communities whose vulnerabilities impair autonomous decision making. Psychologists are aware of and respect cultural, individual, and role differences, including those based on age, gender, gender identity, race, ethnicity, culture, national origin,

> *religion,* sexual orientation, disability, language, and socioeconomic status and consider these factors when working with members of such groups. Psychologists try to eliminate the effect on their work of biases based on those factors, and they do not knowingly participate in or condone activities of others based upon such prejudices. (p. 1063)

In addition, Section 2.01(b) under Boundaries of Competence reads:

> Where scientific or professional knowledge in the discipline of psychology establishes that an understanding of factors associated with age, gender, gender identity, race, ethnicity, culture, national origin, *religion,* sexual orientation, disability, language, or socioeconomic status is essential for effective implementation of their services or research, *psychologists have or obtain the training, experience, consultation, or supervision necessary to ensure the competence of their services, or they make appropriate referrals,* except as provided in Standard 2.02, Providing Services in Emergencies. (pp. 1063-1064)

There is an ethical mandate for psychologists and marriage and family therapists to take an informed view of religion as a dimension of human diversity. However, it appears that the word is not reaching everyone in the field. Kahle (1995) found that practicing psychologists did not always act in accordance with ethical guidelines they did not personally see as important. In ethical discussions related to the integration of spirituality and psychotherapy, it's helpful to differentiate between ethical guidelines, theory, and practice.

According to the ethical guidelines and codes of conduct for the mental health profession, do you see support for the belief that "It is unethical to talk about God, spirituality, or religion in therapy"? Do these guidelines seem to support the notion that "Since there is a danger of imposing one's own values regarding God, spirituality, or religion onto the client, it is therefore ethical to avoid such discussions in therapy"? Finally, where is the support for the assumption, "Since therapy is not religion, it is therefore ethical to avoid discussing issues related to religion with your clients"? In fact, let's take this discussion one step further. Is it unethical to talk about race, gender, age, or ethnicity in therapy? Since it's theoretically possible to impose one's own values regarding gender, race, age, and ethnicity onto clients, is it ethical to avoid discussing these topics in therapy? The following exercise expands upon this discussion.

Self-Reflexercise

Imagine, for a moment, that a client walks into your office for the first time. He's a young Hispanic man who reports he recently told his very traditional Hispanic family that he's gay. He reports that he's seeking some therapeutic support related to coping with their reaction upon finding out that he's gay. You agree to meet with the client on an ongoing basis as long as you can focus on issues other than those related to ethnicity and sexual orientation.

How do you think your state ethics board would respond? Furthermore, when you get called in front of the ethics board, imagine that you present the following reasons for your position. "First, it's unethical to talk about these issues in therapy. Next, since there's a risk of imposing my own values onto the client, it's unethical for me to talk about the issues my client wanted to talk about. Finally, since 'race' and 'sexual orientation' are not synonyms for therapy, I therefore don't have to talk about these issues in therapy." We propose that the ethics board would not believe this was the best day of your professional life. In fact, anyone presenting this kind of argument to an ethics board would certainly be reprimanded.

Erroneously assuming that a conversation related to spiritual and/or religious issues in therapy is unethical is the same type of flawed, extremist thinking that therapists often have to address when working with their clients. It's not only "not always unethical" to talk about issues related to religion and spirituality with clients in therapy, the evidence suggests that it's unethical to avoid such discussions. In fact, *avoiding a discussion of spirituality in therapy based on a fear of imposing one's values is also a value imposition.* Once the subject is broached in therapy, an ethical therapist may choose to refer a client to another therapist who has expertise in this area, but this does not constitute avoidance. Therefore, ethical guidelines give the ethical therapist two options in the case of addressing religion as an issue of human diversity to be respected in therapy. The therapist shall either seek to become competent in this area or he or she shall refer the client to a colleague who is competent in this area. Note that ignoring or minimizing the importance of religion/spirituality in the life of the client are not viable options for ethical therapists.

This doesn't mean that it's always appropriate to address spiritual issues in therapy or that a therapist should always address spiritual issues in each session. Neither does this mean that if a therapist is talking about spiritual issues with his or her client this discussion is therefore automatically an ethical one. However, what this does mean is that the question of whether or not a therapist is acting in an ethical manner during a therapeutic conversation should be reserved for the manner in which the topic is being addressed, rather than exclusively for the topic itself. In other words, whether a particular conversation is ethical is more context dependent than content dependent. Understanding this concept doesn't require the intellectual acumen and expertise of a rocket scientist, nor does it fall within the realms of uncharted territory. We're simply suggesting that therapists apply the same standards toward the issues of spirituality and religion that they do toward other issues they're confronted with in therapy.

Let's extend this discussion further through the use of the following example.

Self-Reflexercise

Imagine that you walk into an observation room with a one-way mirror and the first words you hear from the therapist on the other side of the mirror are, "How many orgasms have you had during the past week?" What thoughts would enter your mind? Could that question be demonstrative of unethical or inappropriate behavior on the part of a therapist? Is it necessarily demonstrative of unethical behavior on the part of a therapist? What if the therapist was working with a client who had been having problems with a sexual dysfunction but had just reported some major progress over the past week? Would it be competent or incompetent on the part of the therapist to discuss issues related to the client's presenting problem? Furthermore, would it not be incumbent on the part of the therapist to be respectful of the client regarding how he or she addresses issues that the client has expressed a desire to address in therapy?

Can it be difficult, at times, to talk about sexual issues in therapy? Is it possible for a therapist to impose his or her own preferences related to sexual intimacy onto the client? Is the word "sex" synonymous with "therapy"? Have you ever heard anyone make the case on ethical grounds that they are free to avoid discussing issues related to sexual intimacy with a client who wants to integrate this topic into therapy? Have you ever heard a therapist report that he or she was told in training that it's unethical to talk about issues related to sexual intimacy in therapy? This double standard nurtures confusion, especially in light of the characteristics of the cultures in which we practice.

IN GOD DOES THIS DIVERSE CULTURE TRUST?

The percentage of Americans who affirm a belief in God has remained around 95 percent since studies first addressed this question in 1944 (Gallup, 2001; Gallup Organization, 1985) (see Table 4.1). Approximately 80 percent of Americans believe in a personal God, a God who answers prayer and watches over humankind (Gallup, 2001). Approximately 90 percent of Americans report that they engage in prayer, a percentage that has been consistent over the past half-century (Gallup, 1999). About 75 percent of Americans report that they pray on a daily basis (Gallup, 1999). The majority of adults

TABLE 4.1. Spiritual/religious beliefs and practices in the United States

Spiritual/Religious Beliefs and Practices	Proportion of Americans	Source
Believe in God	95%	Gallup, 2001
Believe in a personal God	80%	Gallup, 2001
Engage in prayer	90%	Gallup, 1999
Pray on a daily basis	75%	Gallup, 1999
State a religious preference	92%	Gallup, 2001
Religion is very or fairly important in life	86%	Gallup News Service, 2002
Member of church or synagogue	66%	Gallup News Service, 2002
Religion can answer all or most of today's problems	63%	Gallup News Service, 2001
Believe Bible is the actual or inspired word of God	76%	Gallup News Service, 2001
Desire some type of religious education for their children	90%	Hoge, 1996

report that they pray to a Supreme Being, such as Jesus Christ, God, the Lord, or Jehovah, and only 1 percent report their prayers are New Age in nature, such as to a cosmic force, the "god within," or the "inner self" (Gallup, 1999). For those professionals in the mental health community who are sheltered from the pulse of our culture by the walls of academia, these numbers may be quite surprising.

Studies also suggest that a large majority of Americans affiliate themselves with, and participate in, organized religion. According to Gallup (2001), 92 percent of Americans stated a religious preference. The religious preferences of Americans, as they defined themselves, were as follows: 56 percent Protestant, 25 percent Catholic, 8 percent none, 5 percent undesignated, 3 percent other specific, 2 percent Jewish, and 1 percent Mormon (Gallup, 2001).

However, the importance of this issue goes well beyond simple identification with a particular religion. *Approximately one-third of Americans reported that religious commitment was the most important aspect of their lives* (Bergin, Payne, and Richards, 1996). More recently, the Gallup News Service (2002) found that 86 percent of Americans surveyed reported that religion is very or fairly important in their lives. In another study, 63 percent of those surveyed think religion "can answer all or most of today's problems" (Gallup News Service, 2001). Also, 66 percent of Americans surveyed reported being a member of a church or a synagogue (Gallup News Service, 2002). At least 90 percent desire some type of religious education for their children (Hoge, 1996). Furthermore, the Gallup News Service (2001) reported that 76 percent believe that the Bible is either the actual word of God to be taken literally (27 percent) or it is the inspired word of God (49 percent). Cognizant of the influence that spirituality and religion have on American culture, renowned psychology professor Dr. Edward Shafranske (1996) concluded, "Religion appears to be a significant cultural institution, providing meaning, affiliation, and support for many individuals" (p. 150).

MULTIPLE RELIGIOUS CULTURES WITHIN AMERICAN CULTURE

Nancy Boyd-Franklin (1989) suggested that there may be an inseparability between culture and religion. She states, "After the family and extended family, the church is the most common source of help to Black people" (p. 82). She notes that the African-American community church has been an important source for providing young people with role models, developing leadership in the African-American community, and providing support for coping with the intense pain of racism and discrimination (Boyd-Franklin, 1989). In a study on caregivers for relatives with dementia, Segall and Wykle (1988-1989) found that 65 percent of the African Americans interviewed reported prayer and faith were utilized to help them cope with their circumstance. Boyd-Franklin (1989) suggests that if a therapist does not understand that some African-American clients frame concerns in religious terms, a value clash may result with the clients terminating therapy:

> Training in the mental health fields largely ignores the role of spirituality and religious beliefs in the development of the psyche and in its impact on family life. In the treatment of Black families, this oversight is a serious one. (p. 78)

Boyd-Franklin's point may be expanded to include the treatment of religious families and/or individuals of other cultures as well.

Religion and spirituality also play extremely important roles in the lives of many Hispanic families (Sue and Sue, 1990). Approximately 25 to 35 percent of American Catholics are Hispanic (Hoge, 1996). Participating in prayer, Mass, and other religious activities often provide Hispanic families with a source of comfort during stressful times. For many, religious convictions are related to the belief that sacrifice on earth is helpful to salvation (Sue and Sue, 1990).

Therapists who have worked with gay, lesbian, or bisexual clients know that it's essentially inevitable that a conversation will arise about God or the influence that religion has had on their lives. In fact, therapists need to have an understanding of the various struggles that gays, lesbians, and bisexuals are confronted with as they incorporate their sexual identity and orientation within the existing context of a spiritual and/or religious identity (Buchanan et al., 2001).

McGoldrick, Pearce, and Giordano (1982) report that religious differences between Anglo-American groups are often marginalized and represent hidden cultures. For example, Anglo clients who are German-American Lutherans, Irish-American Catholics, or Polish-American Jews have unique values and customs that would likely influence the course of therapy (McGoldrick, Pearce, and Giordano, 1982). Also, Melissa Elliott (Griffith, 1995a) states that when talking with someone from the deep South who is dealing with the influence of pain in his or her life, "you can be nearly certain that some talk of the Lord will come up" (p. 4). Elliott (Griffith, 1995a) asserted that there are important distinctions within the southern Christian stories. Therefore, Elliott suggested that it is important for therapists to listen carefully to every client's unique God narrative.

> Despite all of this, training in the clinical professions is almost bereft of content that would engender an appreciation of religious variables in psychological functioning. Race, gender, and ethnic origin now receive deserved attention, but religion is still an orphan in academia. (Bergin, 1983, p. 171)

Although Bergin made this statement some twenty years ago, research has demonstrated that his words, unfortunately, still accurately describe the training practices in psychology programs today (Schulte, Skinner, and Claiborn, 2002).

In a recent study of training directors or other representatives of counseling psychology programs in the United States, 69 percent who responded reported that the following statement was *false:* "Religious/spiritual issues are regularly discussed as issues of diversity in the program." In response to another statement, "Religious/spiritual diversity is considered as important in the program as other kinds of diversity, such as ethnicity or gender," 65 percent of these respondents reported this statement was *false* (Schulte, Skinner, and Claiborn, p. 124). Needless to say, these findings are alarming and somewhat confusing in light of the wishes of many diverse clients and the ethical appropriateness for such conversations to take place in psychotherapy.

If it's ethical to talk about spiritual issues in therapy, and research involving therapists indicates that clients often bring up such issues in therapy, then why are therapists reporting that they are getting messages in their training that discourage them from discussing God in therapy? Furthermore, if research suggests that clients often initiate discussions of spiritual issues in therapy, and ethical guidelines suggest that therapists need to have a working knowledge of human diversity issues, including religion, so they can work effectively with their clients, would it not be reasonable to assume that this would make the integration of spirituality and psychotherapy a high priority in the training institutions of our world? If not, where would therapists learn how to appropriately have therapeutic conversations about spirituality and/or religion? With these questions in mind, we wonder, What is being done in the training and education institutions to help therapists appropriately handle the issues of spirituality and/or religion when clients introduce the topic during the course of therapy?

Chapter 5

The Influence of the Pink Elephants in the Ivory Tower

Education is what survives when what has been learned has been forgotten.

B. F. Skinner
in *New Scientist*

BRIEF POINT OF CLARIFICATION

We realize that numerous schools and accredited training programs utilize Christian counseling approaches to training, and we support the existence of such programs, although neither of us attended one. Our intent is to address the broader group, all members within the mental health community. The ethical codes and guidelines within our community were not created solely for Christian counselors and Christian counseling educators/trainers. The existing mandates are directed at all mental health professionals, therapists, academics, trainers, and educators. We've heard some within our field say things such as, "That's why we have Christian counselors. They're addressing it, so that need's getting met. Hence, the rest of us don't have to." Needless to say, we could digress and share our thoughts on this type of thinking in a Millerian-type rant for pages. For brevity's sake, let's just say that we think this type of assertion is weaker than a spinachless Popeye. The ethical guidelines are very clear: all educators, counselors, and therapists have a responsibility to seek out education and training related to the competent integration of religious issues in their work.

EDUCATION AND TRAINING

Shafranske (1996) states that "education and training within the area of psychology and religion appears to be very limited; the vast majority of therapists report that religious issues were rarely, if ever, addressed" (p. 160). In one survey, 85 percent of clinical psychologists described themselves as having minimal or no training in religion and psychology (Shafranske and Maloney, 1990). This finding should not be surprising, since a review of introductory psychology textbooks discovered that there were no references relating to the possibility that spiritual factors could be real and most did not contain the words *religion* or *God* in the index (Bergin, 1980a).

A study by Kelly (1994) of department heads at 343 counselor education programs found that 287 of these programs had no course on religious/spiritual issues with regard to counseling. Furthermore, 250 of these programs had no course component addressing religious/ spiritual topics in counseling. The majority of programs supplied little or no supervision on spiritual/religious issues related to either the therapist in training or the client. State-affiliated training programs were significantly less likely to give attention to these issues than were training programs in religious institutions. Approximately 45 percent of the respondents viewed religion and spirituality as either very important or important in preparing counselors for therapy, and approximately 41 percent deemed them somewhat important. Based on these results, Kelly concludes that there was a discrepancy between perceptions of importance and actual attention given to these matters in training.

Sollod (1992) proposed that when training programs and universities ignore the religious aspects of a trainee, they negate a potentially important part of his or her life. Stander and colleagues (1994) suggest:

> Students learn to compartmentalize their religious learning from the rest of their education. To be sure, organized religion can be misused, and certain religious dictums can become straightjackets. However, . . . to ignore the religious is to truncate the process of education and therapy in potentially limiting ways. (p. 34)

Bergin (1980a) asserted that addressing these issues in training does not necessitate proreligious attitudes but does require openness to nontraditional alternatives.

In a sample of clinical training directors of psychology internship centers, 72 percent of the respondents reported that they reviewed case studies where spiritual/religious issues were addressed (Lannert, 1992). The respondents reported that spiritual issues were addressed in approximately 60 percent of initial intakes. Furthermore, 76 percent of the respondents reported that spiritual and/or religious topics were dealt with in clinical case presentations. Lannert suggested that these percentages were remarkable, since over 80 percent of the respondents claimed to have no working knowledge of the psychology of religion.

We hypothesize that many professionals who claim to have a working knowledge of the psychology of religion pursued nontraditional avenues to obtain such training and education. For example, Stander and colleagues (1994) suggested that professional journals have recently become more active in education of professionals with regard to the integration of religion and therapy. Bergin (1980a) suggested that articles submitted for publication that related to religion and therapy were censored from professional journals. However, a number of journals, such as the *Journal of Marriage and Family Therapy, Counseling and Values,* and the *Journal of Counseling Psychology,* now openly address the integration of spiritual issues and therapy.

In addition, presentations at professional conferences on the integration of spirituality and psychotherapy have been on the rise in recent years. These changes should not be surprising considering that many professionals have stated a desire for more formalized training in this area (Shafranske, 1996). Research results indicate that 62 percent of psychologists surveyed reported that clinical training and supervision in dealing with spiritual and religious issues with clients would be helpful, and 54 percent appraised the psychology of religion as beneficial in the education of clinical psychologists (Shafranske, 1996). Thus, Shafranske (1996) suggested that the avoidance of these issues in training forced many clinicians to rely on personal training rather than professional training when discussions of religious issues would arise in therapy. Although many conferences and journals have responded to the ethical mandate to provide competent training in this area of human diversity, research has unfortunately demonstrated that Shafranske's assertion is still very true today.

A more recent study (Schulte, Skinner, and Claiborn, 2002) of training directors and other representatives from forty counseling psychology training programs in the United States found that 82 percent of these programs offered no courses with a specifically religious or spiritual theme. Furthermore, 61 percent of these programs offered either no course (33 percent) or only one course (28 percent) that included any religious or spiritual content at all. Although 90 percent of the respondents believed that faculty members were open to research on religious/spiritual issues, and 83 percent of the respondents believed faculty members were willing to supervise student research on religious/spiritual issues, something very interesting emerged. In response to, "Faculty members in the program are expected to be knowledgeable about various religious/spiritual traditions," 91 percent of these same respondents indicated that this statement was *false*. Perhaps a better question than whether these faculty members are "open" to supervise research in this area would be whether or not these faculty members are "competent" to supervise research in this area.

Unfortunately, this wasn't the only unsettling finding in this study. In response to, "Knowledge of various religious/spiritual traditions is considered an important part of a supervisor's expertise in the program," 76 percent of the respondents indicated this statement was *false*. In response to, "Knowledge of various religious/spiritual traditions is considered an important part of a therapist's expertise in the program," 72 percent of the respondents indicated this statement was *false*. Needless to say, it was no surprise to discover that 87 percent of these respondents indicated *false* to the statement, "Students in the program learn about religious/spiritual development."

Although many professionals may claim that they're open to training and/or willing to be involved in training in this area, actions, or perhaps we should say the lack of their actions, speak louder than their words. Indeed, to aspire to act ethically is not the equivalent of acting ethically.

REACTIVE VERSUS PROACTIVE TRAINING

After studying these findings in great depth, we developed two terms to differentiate between the types of training that either are or are not occurring in training institutions. The research indicates that training institutions are much more involved in "reactive training" than they are in "proactive training." With regard to training in the mental health care field, we describe proactive training as training that specializes in preparing therapists, in advance, for issues and/or situations that may arise during the course of therapy. This type of training is employed in the hope that individuals will be better prepared to address these issues, if they should arise in therapy, in an appropriate and healthy manner. On the other hand, we describe reactive training as training that specializes in responding to a particular issue and/or situation that has already arisen in therapy. This type of training is employed in the hope that individuals will be better prepared in the future to more appropriately handle the issue or situation to which they have *already* had to respond in therapy.

For simplicity's sake, let's simply focus on the findings of the Kelly (1994) and Lannert (1992) studies to further illustrate the differences between these two types of training. As reported earlier, Kelly (1994) found that 287 of the 343 counselor education programs surveyed had no course on religious/spiritual issues and counseling and 250 of the programs did not even have a course component on religious/spiritual issues and counseling. It appears, therefore, that the overwhelming majority of counselor education programs did not utilize proactive training to help prepare their counselors in training to appropriately address spiritual issues when they arise in counseling. These findings raise interesting questions on their own. However, when reviewed in conjunction with the Lannert study's findings, an interesting process comes to light. Recall Lannert (1992) found, in a sample of clinical training directors, that 76 percent reported spiritual/religious issues were addressed in case presentations. At first glance, this appears to be an encouraging percentage. However, on deeper examination, this raises concerns for at least three reasons.

First, 80 percent of these clinical training directors claimed no working knowledge of the psychology of religion. This makes sense considering the antispirituality/antireligious bias that has existed in the field of psychology for years. The bottom line is that many of the trainers in the mental health field were never trained in this area themselves.

Second, beyond the content level and looking at the process level of these studies, we noticed something else of concern. Where did 76 percent of the clinical training directors in the Lannert study report that spiritual/religious issues were addressed? In case presentations. What do we know about case presentations? Although they vary in some ways, generally speaking these presentations are based on cases in which counselors and/or counselors in training are working with actual clients. Counselors often choose certain cases to present to their colleagues and/or supervisors because they are either challenged by the case and/or they think such cases are an example of some excellent work they've done. Regardless, they are presenting something that has come up in therapy. This type of training would fall within the category of reactive training. So, when the topic is brought up in case presentations, research suggests that many of the supervisors lack any knowledge with regard to how to address these issues in an appropriate, healthy, and competent manner. This is alarming.

Third, what if no counselor in training ever brought up spiritual issues in training? It is possible that some people could actually go through training with spiritual and religious issues never being overtly addressed in an ethical and/or helpful manner by an instructor.

We believe that both proactive and reactive training are valuable and can be helpful. We simply wonder why, with regard to the issues of spirituality, religion, and counseling, so much of the training appears to take place as a reaction to what is brought up in therapy, rather than being addressed proactively in training? Assuming that hypotheses, theories, and empirical research may not be sufficient for some people to grasp the implications of this problem, we decided to add one more piece to the puzzle. We thought it might be helpful to share a real-life example of the dangers associated with training institutions that rely on reactive training to address religious and spiritual issues in therapy.

SUPERVISING WITH A BACK-PEW DRIVER

After completing a recent training seminar, we were approached by a counselor in training. "Susan" told us about a recent supervision experience in which she had done a case presentation involving a male client with whom she was currently working. Susan said that the client had reported feeling down, regretting something he had recently done. As the client talked about this issue, he reported to Susan that he was a Christian and was concerned about what God thought of him because of what he had done. Susan told us that she had decided how to address this issue with her client based on a discussion she had in her supervision practicum class. She reported that she had asked her supervising professor what to do. Susan's professor had said that since she was not a religious person, she would defer to a student in the class who was known to be a religious person. Susan said that her fellow student suggested that she could easily address her client's situation by informing the client that his view of God was too big. "Tell him that God is not really concerned with the small things in life and not to worry about it." Susan reported that the class and her professor agreed that this advice might prove to be effective. Then Susan asked, "What do you think of doing that?" We'll save our full response until a later section, but let's just say at this point that we were floored by a number of issues within this brief, real-life example from 2001. It demonstrates the dangers of reactive training in the hands of individuals who are ill prepared to advise on such matters.

Our search to determine some of the contributing factors to where we are today, with regard to the integration of spirituality and psychotherapy, sometimes leaves us feeling as though we are traveling in circles. Nevertheless, we continue our process of questioning in the hope of decreasing the influence of confusion in our lives. If therapists report that clients want to discuss spiritual issues in therapy, and if clinical trainers report that they have no working knowledge of the psychology of religion, and if therapists report that they would like more formalized training, why is the training offered in the mental health field often limited to reactive training in training programs or the reading of certain journals and/or attendance in CEU seminars, all of which are based on the professional's own initiative and thus selective bias? In other words, why in the world are we where we are today with regard to how we are addressing the integration of spirituality and psychotherapy?

At a training workshop we conducted in February 2002, we divided the participants into small groups of four to five members after presenting the previously mentioned research findings related to the current state of training in the mental health field. We asked these professionals to brainstorm as to why they thought the overwhelming majority of the training institutions were not overtly addressing the issues of spirituality and religion in spite of the ethical mandates. The two most often cited reasons for the poor training in this area were, "It's not politically correct to talk about spirituality, religion, or God" and "Spirituality is a personal matter, hence perhaps we shouldn't talk about it in therapy." Many of the participants erupted in laughter when I (PK) responded to the last assertion by asking, "Exactly what issues do we talk about in therapy that aren't personal issues?" Yet we agreed that many of us had felt the impact of the covert yet powerfully threatening hypothetical construct known as political correctness.

After studying research findings and discussing this subject at great length, we've come to the conclusion that a number of factors, in addition to the fear of the politically correct police, have contributed to the current state of training in this area. We discovered one of these factors during a conversation we had a few years ago. Although we attended different training institutions, John and I discovered that our training paths had been identical in one important way. We discovered that we had an instructor in common. As we discussed this instructor, we realized that he had influenced both of us with regard to our thinking on the subject of religion and psychology.

Regardless of whether this instructor was one of your professors, we think you may be able to better understand where we're coming from if we share with you some of this instructor's comments on religion and psychological health. Therefore, we invite you to participate in another reflexive exercise based on encounters we both had with this instructor. (Again, we encourage you to pause and think after each of the following questions before going on.)

Self-Reflexercise

Imagine that you're seated in a classroom on the first day of a new semester awaiting the arrival of your professor. You're eagerly awaiting his arrival because you have heard glowing reports about this instructor's intelligence and insight into psychological processes. In fact, you're very excited as he enters the classroom. Soon after he begins to discuss his insight into the psychology of human beings, you discover that he is an excellent lecturer. You quickly realize why others have spoken of him as they have. Throughout his lecture, you're sitting at the edge of your seat captivated by his ideas on a wide range of psychological topics. Then, toward the end of the lecture, he shifts the discussion to the topic of religious beliefs. Right after he states that he does not believe in "the Christian myth," he completes this section of his lecture by saying,

> The whole thing [religion] is so patently infantile, so foreign to reality, that to anyone with a friendly attitude to humanity it is painful to think that the great majority of mortals will never be able to rise above this view of life.
>
> God at bottom is nothing but an exalted father.

As you hear this, what is your first thought? What are you feeling? Do you agree with his assertions? If so, why? If not, why? Now imagine that you look around your classroom and notice that many of your fellow students are smiling as they nod their heads in agreement. How would you feel? Next, your instructor closes his briefcase and walks out of the room to the sound of appreciative applause. What might this lead you to think?

The next week, you hear many of your fellow classmates talking about the instructor's amazing insight into religion. For the purpose of further exploration, let's assume that you agree with your fellow students and are extremely impressed with your instructor's insight into religious thinking. You're discussing his ideas with your classmates when you notice a number of students rushing across the campus toward your university's newspaper stand, where many students have gathered. You join the mass of students, who, in disbelief, are standing together as they read an article about your psychology instructor. You snatch up the last paper just before another student and read the following article.

Instructor Faces New Charges
After a Patient Dies a Cocaine Addict

One of our university's most renowned instructors recently admitted that he himself has used cocaine for some time and has even given the drug to his patients, family, and friends. The psychology instructor was unavailable for comment because he's currently recovering from his thirty-third operation for cancer of the palate and jaw. His physician commented briefly about his nicotine addiction, adding, "I just hope we can get him to decrease his smoking below his current average of twenty cigars per day." Now, one of his trusted colleagues and friends has accused him of having an extramarital affair with his own wife's sister. Some have wondered whether the instructor might say in his defense, "It was a completely free association since she had penis envy." More details will be reported as they emerge.

If all of these claims were true, would you question the psychological health of your instructor? If so, why? If not, why? If these charges were true, would you question your instructor's theories about psychological health and religion? If so, why? If not, why? If all of these claims were true, would you wonder whether your instructor was aware of his own issues or had blind spots larger than a windowless Suburban? If so, why? If not, why?

Obviously, we're trying to have some fun in this process. However, we encourage you to not allow our attempts at humor minimize the seriousness of our questions. For indeed, all of us are left to wonder what importance we should place on the work of the "father of Psychology," Sigmund Freud. However, make no mistake, his ideas about religion and psychology have influenced many individuals in the history of psychology and remain a powerful source of influence on many professionals involved in training today. We believe that Freud's views, the views of some others, and the irreligious beliefs of therapists have all helped to create an environment in many of the institutions of higher education in which "institutional aspiritualism" is condoned by being either passively ignored or actively denied. This covert process of supporting aspiritualistic thought is very common and pervasive, regardless of whether those within the ivory tower of academia own it or not. As the enigmatic Ricky Fitts, played by Wes Bentley, in the Academy Award winning film, *American Beauty* (1999) said, "Never underestimate the power of denial." This reality is, of course, nothing new.

Universities incline wits to sophistry and affectation.

Francis Bacon

Based on what we have explored, it seems wise to address the question, "Historically speaking, did everyone agree with Freud's beliefs about the psychology of religious beliefs?"

Chapter 6

Can We Agree That Many Have Disagreed?

People seem not to see that their opinion of the world is also a confession of character.

Ralph Waldo Emerson
"Worship" in *The Conduct of Life,* 1860

There is disagreement within the mental health field regarding the relationship between religion, spirituality, and psychological health. We've encountered many professionals across the United States over the past several years who approached us after our presentations and said things such as, "I had no idea about the history of psychology and religion" or "I never knew that any of the historical figures in the mental health care fields actually had any positive views about religion or spirituality." We've also been approached by numerous graduate students who have said things such as, "It's not safe in my training program to talk about spiritual issues in therapy." In each of these instances, it appeared that a tremendous burden had been lifted from their shoulders when they discovered that not every psychotherapist views religion as a form of illusionary wish fulfillment and/or it wasn't necessarily unethical or inappropriate to talk about spirituality in therapy. We can relate to this sense of relief because we had similar experiences after exploring the history of thought in this area. In fact, a review of historical perspectives proves to be not only relieving but also quite enlightening.

A VERY BRIEF HISTORY OF THE INTEGRATION OF SPIRITUALITY, RELIGION, AND THERAPY

Andrews (1987) asserts that the concept of psychotherapy can be traced to Plato's (424-347 B.C.) attempt to use a pragmatic code of moral values to relieve the emotional problems besetting the military and economic deterioration of Athens. Although Plato did not use the term *psychotherapy,* he referred to justice as the orderly application of ethical discipline to enhance the natural healing power of the rational soul (Andrews, 1987). Plato believed it was possible to treat even the severest afflictions through the use of an ethical therapy that recommended honesty in a person's family and business affairs. He also thought it was important to balance respect for others' opinions with devotion for the convictions of a person's own heart (Andrews, 1987). The influence of Plato's ethical therapy was, and remains, evident in the work of many prominent doctors and philosophers over the centuries (Andrews, 1987).

Religious counselors were a vital part of the early Israelite courts (Strunk, 1985). In addition, religious leaders in the Christian Church have always been involved in the counseling and guidance of their congregational members (Strunk, 1985). Strunk (1985) suggests that, "Pastoral counseling is as old as the church and as new as the birth of psychoanalysis" (p. 14).

A review of the NIV (New International Version) Exhaustive Concordance (Goodrick and Kohlenberger, 1990) of the Holy Bible revealed that counseling is a prominent topic in both the Old and New Testaments. The terms *counsel, counsels,* and *counselor* appear fifty-six times. *Counsel* or *counsels* are utilized numerous times to describe one of the means by which individuals can receive assistance from God. Furthermore, the term *counselor* is a specific title employed to refer to God on five occasions in the Old and New Testaments. For example, when speaking of the Messiah, Isaiah wrote, "For to us a child is born, to us a son is given, and the government will be on his shoulders. And he will be called Wonderful Counselor, Mighty God, Everlasting Father, Prince of Peace" (Isaiah 9:6, NIV). Therefore, individuals from both Jewish and Christian traditions might contend that the idea of utilizing counseling to nurture psychological health has existed from the inception of human history.

The Latin word *psychologia* was first utilized around 1524 by Marko Marulic, a Croatian philosopher, ethicist, and poet who is considered the father of Croatian literature, to refer to "one of the subdivisions of pneumatology, the science of spiritual beings and substances" (Vande Kemp, 1996, p. 72). The resulting three subdivisions were "natural theology (concerning God), angelology/demonology (concerning the intermediate spirits), and psychology (concerning the human spirit)" (Vande Kemp, 1996, p. 72). In the eighteenth century, Von Wolff made a distinction between empirical and rational psychology that eventually led to theoretical psychometrics and paved the way for scientific psychology (Vande Kemp, 1996). Dr. Hendrika Vande Kemp (1996) suggests that:

> Psychologists trained in the dominant historical tradition of the 20th century may be startled to learn that psychology and religion have historically been this inextricably intertwined. . . . The connection is also inevitable because it is virtually impossible to make a clear distinction between pneuma (the spirit, or religious aspect of the person) and psyche (the soul, or the psychological). (p. 72)

Berliner (1992) notes that one of the original meanings for the Latin term *therapeia* was "soul healing." Although theoretically both religion and psychology conclude that they can have a healing influence on the human psyche (Miller, 1992), opinions about integrating the religious with the psychological have seemed to dichotomize toward the polar ends of a pro-integration and against-integration continuum (Carter and Narramore, 1979).

THE PSYCHOLOGY OF RELIGION

Many of the founders of American psychology integrated religion and psychology (Gorsuch, 1988). For instance, G. Stanley Hall, in addition to being the first president of the American Psychological Association and receiving the first PhD in psychology, was very interested in the study of religious psychology (Gorsuch, 1988). In 1904, he established the *American Journal of Religious Psychology* (later known as *The Journal of Religious Psychology*) (Vande Kemp, 1992). Even before this, Hall taught the psychology of religion in

1887-1888 at Johns Hopkins University. At Clark University, he taught at least one course on religious psychology annually after 1900, except from 1913 to 1915, with course titles such as Psychology of Jesus, Psychology of Religion, and Psychology of Religion and Christianity (Vande Kemp, 1992). In fact, over 10 percent of Hall's own publications were on religious psychology (Vande Kemp, 1992).

William James, the Boston medical professor who founded Harvard University's psychology department, was also interested in the integration of psychology and religion (Andrews, 1987). In his classic book *The Varieties of Religious Experience* ([1902] 1929), James asserts:

> I am neither a theologian, nor a scholar learned in the history of religions, nor an anthropologist. Psychology is the only branch of learning in which I am particularly versed. To the psychologist the religious propensities of man must be at least as interesting as any other of the facts pertaining to his mental constitution. (p. 4)

In this work, James not only declared his belief that the study of religious experience is worthy of psychology but also proposed that religion could be a pathway to human excellence. James asserted that levels of human excellence that are otherwise unobserved may be realized when intellect and religious inspiration are blended in equally large measure. He states:

> Religious feeling is thus an absolute addition to the subject's range of life. It gives him a new sphere of power. . . . This sort of happiness in the absolute and everlasting is what we find nowhere but in religion. It is parted off from all mere animal happiness, all mere enjoyment of the present, by that element of solemnity. (James, [1902] 1929, p. 48)

James believed, therefore, that religion can potentially play a useful role in helping individuals procure psychological excellence.

Carl Jung viewed religion as a way to wholeness (Wulff, 1996). According to Jung, archetypes actively help to re-create past experiences from the collective unconscious in the present (Jung, [1954] 1968). For Jung, the primary goal of this complex dynamic was individuation or self-realization, the lifelong process of integration and differentiation that eventually makes the individual whole (Jung, [1954] 1968). Although Jung often defined religion as the experience of the numinous, or Holy, he also believed that self-realization could be facilitated through participation in religious rituals (Jung, [1932] 1969). Jung ([1932] 1969) specifically addressed the importance of religious content and implications for therapy in the following statement:

> Among all my patients in the second half of life—that is to say, over thirty-five—there has not been one whose problem in the last resort was not that of finding a religious outlook on life. It is safe to say that every one of them fell ill because he had lost what the living religions of every age have given to their followers, and none of them has been really healed who did not regain his religious outlook. (p. 334)

Thus he suggests that each client's religious outlook influenced his or her mental health.

In the 1950s, Erik Erikson, famous for advancing a human developmental model based on eight stages of psychosocial development, suggested that religion could serve as a foundation for human beings, providing them with hope and wisdom (Wulff, 1996). According to Erikson ([1950] 1963), religion's deepest roots could be traced to the maternal matrix of infancy, since religion connects with the most fundamental needs, longings, and fears of human beings. He asserted that religious ritualization provides people with a sense of higher meaning, an understanding of human existence, and serves to regulate impulsivity. Erikson acknowledged that the use of coercive dogmatism in religion could potentially produce pathological distortions in human beings, such as self-righteous or moralistic legalism and narcissistic elitism. In spite of the potential for pathological distortions, Erikson maintained that religion is essential for the attainment of maturity in human beings. Although recognizing that religion can potentially be both helpful and harmful to clients, Erikson employed an early competency-based analysis of the psychology of religion. However, many of his colleagues within the field approached the psychology of religion from a more problem-focused perspective.

THE PATHOLOGIZING OF RELIGION

Sigmund Freud also believed that the roots of religious beliefs and practices could be traced to infancy (Wulff, 1996). However, unlike Erikson, Freud asserted that religious beliefs were constructions of infantile wish fulfillment (Freud, [1927] 1961). Freud referred to religious beliefs and belief systems as "illusions, fulfillments of the oldest, strongest, and most urgent wishes of mankind" ([1927] 1961, p. 30). He described religious rituals as obsessive symptoms of neurosis (Freud, [1927] 1961). In *Totem and Taboo,* Freud (1938) asserts that every religion is marked by a longing for the father.

> However, psychoanalytic investigation of the individual teaches with especial emphasis that god in every case is modelled after the father and that our personal relation to god is dependent upon our relation to our physical father, fluctuating and changing with him, and that god at bottom is nothing but an exalted father. (pp. 919-920)

Since the father is also an object of resentment, guilt, and fear, religious resolution of the Oedipus complex occurs as a result of obedient submission to God, the projected infantile father figure. There-

IN THE VALUE-FREE OFFICE OF DR. FREUD

fore, Freud suggested that religion was an illusion because it was based on wish fulfillment rather than on reason and/or observation. He argued that individuals would only be able to mature past this infantile stage by abandoning religion and its teachings and relying instead on reason and science (Freud, [1927] 1961).

In the 1950s, B. F. Skinner insisted that religious behavior is no different than other behaviors and exists only because the behavior has been followed by reinforcing stimuli. Although he viewed behavior as externally controlled, Skinner was critical of traditional religions. He believed traditional religions relied on fiction, negative reinforcement, and the threat of punishment (Skinner, 1953).

As a result of the work of Skinner and other behaviorists such as John B. Watson, increasing numbers of psychologists rejected the importance of internal values and instead focused on manipulating overt behavior (Andrews, 1987). As Gorsuch (1988) states, "hence psychology shifted from the study of the mind and the spirit to the study of behavior" (p. 205). However, just as the work of Skinner and Watson had challenged the psychoanalytic movement, the third force in psychology, humanism, soon lured professional interest away from behaviorism (Hergenhahn, 1992).

OTHER THOUGHTS ALONG THE INTEGRATION CONTINUUM

Carl Rogers (1973), a humanist who believed that exploring the possibility of a higher power was a worthy study for the field of psychology, states:

> There may be a few who will dare to investigate the possibility that there is a lawful reality which is not open to our five senses; a reality in which present, past, and future are intermingled, in which space is not a barrier and time has disappeared. . . . It is one of the most exciting challenges posed to psychology. (p. 386)

However, due in part to the very movement that Rogers inadvertently helped to continue, value-free psychology, the psychology of religion was virtually extinct from 1930 to 1960 (Gorsuch, 1988).

Beginning in the 1960s, integration of psychology and religion occurred in a number of unique ways. For example, divinity schools began teaching courses in value-free psychiatry (Andrews, 1987). Also, the Fuller Theological Seminary established a graduate school in psychology in 1964 (Miller, 1992). Since psychology was now established as a discipline, many psychologists no longer felt the need to avoid topics that resembled philosophy or the study of the mind (Gorsuch, 1988). However, efforts to integrate psychology and religion were in no way considered a mainstream movement. Therefore, in the 1970s, the pro-integration movement was, in large part, advanced in the work of individuals such as M. Scott Peck (1978) and Christian counselors such as James Dobson (1970), Frank Minirth, and Paul Meier (1978).

Throughout the 1980s, the Christian counseling movement continued to grow in popularity as new individuals such as Larry Crabb (1988), Ken Haugk (1984), and Gary Smalley and John Trent (1986) gained popularity for their work. However, the pro-integration movement did not reach mainstream psychology until 1980 when Allen Bergin and Albert Ellis began their infamous values debates (Bergin, Payne, and Richards, 1996). These debates helped to expose one of the other contributing factors to learned avoidance—value-free/value-neutral thinking.

Chapter 7

Valuing Values in Psychotherapy

All sciences are now under the obligation to prepare the ground for the future task of the philosopher, which is to solve the problem of value, to determine the true hierarchy of values.

Friedrich Nietzsche

Although we disagree with Nietzsche's assertion that the true hierarchy of values should be determined by philosophers, we find it interesting to note that even Nietzsche believed it was important to acknowledge the role of values in science. The originator of the "God is dead" statement apparently believed that values are very much alive!

THE REFORMATION OF VALUE-FREE THINKING

Behaviorism added support to the notion advanced by psychoanalysis that it is not only possible, but necessary, for a clinician to leave his or her values behind when entering a therapeutic context (Andrews, 1987). Value-free psychotherapy came from the psychoanalytic view that analysts should be blank screens to amplify transference reactions of clients and intensify projections of client attitudes, values, and beliefs (Patterson, 1989). Carl Rogers' nondirective theory of psychotherapy was also instrumental in advancing the idea of therapist neutrality (Grimm, 1994). However, Rogers himself admitted, as early as 1957, that a therapist could not practice without supplying evidence of personal values and views of human nature (Rogers, 1957). Nonetheless, the notion of value-free or value-neutral psychotherapy remained popular in the field of psychology and went largely unchallenged until 1980 (Bergin, 1980a).

As Martin Luther did in the Christian church centuries before, Allen Bergin challenged the popular beliefs of his time by proposing theses regarding values to his colleagues in the field of psychology. However, Bergin (1980a) chose to express his theses in the *Journal of Consulting and Clinical Psychology* rather than on a church door in Wittenburg, Germany. Bergin (1985) defines values as, "Orienting beliefs about what is good for clients and how that good should be achieved" (p. 99). He proposes the following six theses:

> Thesis 1: Values are an inevitable and pervasive part of psychotherapy. . . . Thesis 2: Not only do theories, techniques, and criteria reveal pervasive value judgments, but outcome data comparing effects of diverse techniques show that technical, value-laden factors pervade professional change processes. . . . Thesis 3: Two broad classes of values are dominant in the mental health professions. Both exclude religious values, and both establish goals for change that frequently clash with theistic systems of belief. . . . Thesis 4: There is a significant contrast between the values of mental health professionals and those of a large proportion of clients. . . . Thesis 5: In light of the foregoing, it would be honest and ethical to acknowledge that we are implementing our own value systems via our professional work and to be more explicit about what we believe while also respecting the value systems of others. . . . Thesis 6: It is our obligation as professionals to translate what we perceive and value intuitively into something that can be openly tested and evaluated. (1980a, pp. 97-101)

Bergin (1980a) asserted that the values in clinical pragmatism and humanistic idealism often contrast with religious values. Also, he demonstrated empirically that even therapists who intended to remain value-free were unsuccessful (Bergin, 1980a). He states that "a value-free approach is impossible" (p. 97). Within the mental health field, a judgment is always made with regard to some type of explicit or implicit standard, which connotes that there is a better and worse (Bergin, 1980a). Thus, since therapists are inevitably moral agents or "secular moralists," he suggested that it was dangerous to ignore the fact that the values of therapists always affect the course of therapy (Bergin, 1980a, p. 97).

After examining three introductory psychology textbooks, Bergin (1980a) noted that there were no references for the possibility that spiritual factors might be a reality. He suggested that conversations about religion had been censored by the field of psychology. Bergin (1980a) concluded that the profession of psychology had championed some personal value systems, such as behaviorism and humanism, while marginalizing other value systems, such as religion. In fact, others have even argued that different schools of psychotherapy are analogous to religions with some of the followers of these schools participating in evangelism, moralism, and dogma (Cade, 1997; Rogers, 1973). Although Bergin's (1980a) ideas were supported by colleagues, such as Albert Bandura, Ellen Berscheid, Karl Menninger, and Carl Rogers, not everyone within the mental health field agreed with Bergin's assertions (Bergin, 1985).

THE BERGIN-ELLIS DEBATES

In response to Bergin's article, Albert Ellis (1980) states, "His six major theses on spiritual values are empirically confirmable and probably valid" (p. 635). However, Ellis (1980) objected to Bergin's article because "he does not properly represent the views of probabilistic atheist clinicians like myself who . . . may well constitute the majority of modern psychotherapists" (p. 635). Ellis (1980) addresses his views about believerism, religion, and psychotherapy when he states:

> Devout, orthodox, or dogmatic religion (or what might be called religiosity) is significantly correlated with emotional disturbance. . . . Religiosity, therefore, is in many ways equivalent to irrational thinking and emotional disturbance. . . . The elegant therapeutic solution to emotional problems is to be quite unreligious and have no degree of dogmatic faith that is unfounded or unfoundable in fact. . . . The less religious they are, the more emotionally healthy they will tend to be. (p. 637)

Also, Ellis (1980) asserted that guilt, which comes from unsuccessfully attempting to follow religious dogma, is harmful. By making their beliefs explicit, Ellis and Bergin began a series of debates on the subject of religious beliefs, therapy, and mental health (Bergin, 1980a,b, 1983, 1985, 1988; Ellis, 1980, 1992a,b).

Bergin (1980b) responded to Ellis's critique by asserting the following:

> Obedience to divine law is, in principle, not different from the concept that exact laws operate in the physical or biological world, and yet is strict obedience to those laws that creates the very possibility for freedom. . . . It is not the endorsing of absolutes that creates problems but the endorsing of them by force and without affection. (p. 644)

Bergin illustrated that Ellis, the founder of rational-emotive therapy (RET), was a victim of his own rationale when he states, "The idea that believerism is emotional disturbance is self-contradictory, for the assertion itself is a form of believerism" (1980b, p. 644). Contrary to Ellis, Bergin asserted that guilt protects society and the psyche in much the same way as pain protects the body (Bergin, 1980b).

In 1988, Bergin demonstrated empirically that value-free and value-neutral therapy were myths (Jensen and Bergin, 1988). Themes emerged from information obtained from a survey of 425 mental health workers. Results demonstrated that psychotherapists endorsed certain traditional values, such as fidelity in marriage, self-control, forgiveness of others, and honesty, as important for a beneficial, mentally healthy lifestyle. Autonomy and striving for achievement were also seen as important values for procuring emotional health. An overwhelming majority of these mental health workers reported that these values *were* "important in guiding and evaluating psychotherapy with all or many clients" (p. 293). As expected, the value theme that was endorsed least often concerned the importance of spirituality and religiosity in psychotherapy. The surveyed therapists apparently considered it more important to keep therapy free from values when those values were spiritual and/or religious values.

Recent Ellis writings suggest that he has become more open about the possible benefits that could result from using religious concepts in therapy (Ellis, 1992a,b). He states:

> I no longer believe that religion creates emotional disturbance but now believe that what I call religiosity—which I define as devout, dogmatic believe [*sic*] in any theological or atheistic creed—tends to lead to neurosis. (p. 38)

Furthermore, Ellis explained that RET supports and teaches a number of religious principles, especially the Christian concept of grace (1992a). Ellis (1992a) acknowledged the potential benefit of using religious concepts in therapy with clients who are sincerely religious. He acknowledged that religiously accommodated RET may be more helpful for religious clients than nonreligiously accommodated RET (Ellis, 1992a). Thus, he recognized that religious members of society could profit from therapy that supported, rather than confronted or ignored, their religious values.

Although Bergin and Ellis disagreed on a number of key points, both men mentioned the values and beliefs of therapists in addressing religious issues in psychotherapy. We wonder, Why would both of these men believe it was important to address the values and beliefs of therapists when discussing the psychological healthiness of religious beliefs? In the end, both men agreed that therapy that was supportive and congruent with a client's religious beliefs could be more helpful than therapy that was not supportive and congruent with a client's religious beliefs. Yet we continue to wonder why two men who passionately disagreed on a number of issues would both believe that the religious beliefs of the person of the therapist were an important issue to address when discussing the psychological health of religious beliefs and the integration of spirituality and psychotherapy. If it was important enough for those two guys, perhaps it should be important enough for these two guys. (Our apologies for the use of "should," Dr. Ellis. We understand that we *should* not use should.)

Chapter 8

In God Do Therapists Trust? In Reality, Better Training Is a Must!

By nature, men are nearly alike; by practice, they get to be wide apart.

Confucius

STUDIES OF RELIGIOUS BELIEFS OF PSYCHOTHERAPISTS

Leuba

The first comprehensive study pertaining to the religious beliefs of psychologists was conducted by Leuba in 1914 (as cited in Leuba, 1950). Leuba's survey sample consisted of scientists across multiple disciplines who were asked whether they believed in a God who answers prayer. Leuba discovered that, across disciplines, psychologists were customarily the least likely to affirm this statement, as 32 percent of the less prominent psychologists and 13 percent of the more distinguished psychologists responded that they did believe in a God who answers prayer. In a 1933 replication of this study, Leuba discovered that 12 percent of the less prominent psychologists and 2 percent of the more distinguished psychologists held this belief.

Digress with us for a moment. The way the findings and implications of these research studies were presented reminded us of an old character played by Kevin Nealon, Mr. Subliminal, on the television show *Saturday Night Live.* We can almost hear Mr. Subliminal saying, "Thirty-two percent of the less prominent psychologists (dipsticks) and thirteen percent of the more distinguished psychologists (correct geniuses) responded that they did believe in a God who answers prayer." Perhaps a spiritual Mr. Subliminal might respond, "Very nice results (antispiritual value-laden methodology), Leuba." Apart from our digression, Leuba's assertion is clear: the smarter and more successful you are, the less spiritual and/or religious you will tend to be.

Bergin and Jensen

Decades after Leuba's studies were published, results from surveys continued to demonstrate that therapists were less committed to traditional values, beliefs, and religious organizations than society at large (Bergin, 1980a). Although more recent research suggests that mental health professionals may be more religious than previously thought (Bergin and Jensen, 1990; Shafranske and Malony, 1990), the religious gap between psychologists and society at large continues to be significant (Bergin, 1991).

Bergin and Jensen (1990) surveyed mental health care professionals to obtain information about their religious preferences and degrees of religious involvement (see Table 8.1). An overwhelming majority (almost 80 percent) of mental health care workers designated some type of religious preference, with Protestants making up the largest group (38 percent). The second most commonly chosen group (20 percent) consisted of those individuals who selected atheist, agnostic, humanist, or none.

TABLE 8.1. Religious preferences of mental health professionals versus general public (in percentages)

Religious Preference	Marriage and Family Therapists (*n* = 118)	Clinical Social Workers (*n* = 106)	Psychiatrists (*n* = 71)	Clinical Psychologists (*n* = 119)	Mental Health Pros (total) (*n* = 414)	General Public[a] (*n* = 1,016)
Protestant	49	40	30	32	38	56
Nonreligious	15	9	24	31	20	8
Jewish	12	22	14	24	18	2
Catholic	14	20	21	9	15	25
Other	9	10	11	5	8	4

Note: This table was adapted from a very similar table used in Bergin (1991). Numbers are percentages from "Religiosity of Psychotherapists: A National Survey" by Bergin and Jensen (1990).
[a]Percentages taken from Gallup (2001).
Nonreligious = Sum of agnostic, atheist, humanist, and none.

Furthermore, results revealed that those psychotherapists who attended church regularly (41 percent) were outnumbered by their colleagues who attended church occasionally or not at all (59 percent). Also, 77 percent of the psychotherapists reported that they try to live their lives according to their religious beliefs. Some 44 percent of the psychotherapists indicated that they endorse having a "religious affiliation in which one actively participates," and 68 percent of the therapists "seek a spiritual understanding of the universe and one's place in it."

The researchers point out that when professional groups were subdivided, results demonstrated significant differences between the professional groups. Clinical psychologists were the least religious psychotherapists, as 33 percent claimed that they attended church regularly and 33 percent described religious faith as the most important thing in their lives. Comparatively, marriage and family therapists were the most religious psychotherapists, as 50 percent claimed that they attended church regularly and 62 percent described religious faith as the most important thing in their lives. Nonetheless, only 29 percent of the therapists surveyed viewed religious matters as important in the treatment of all or many of their clients.

Shafranske and Malony

Shafranske and Malony (1990) surveyed 409 members of American Psychological Association (APA) Division 12 (Clinical Psychology) to obtain information about views of spiritual and religious issues. These participants were asked to select the statement that best represented their personal spiritual orientation from six possible choices. Of those clinical psychologists who responded to this survey, 40 percent supported a "personal, transcendent God" orientation; 30 percent a "transcendent dimension exists in all nature" orientation; 26 percent an "all ideologies are illusions yet meaningful" orientation; 2 percent an "all ideologies are illusions and irrelevant to the world" orientation; and 2 percent did not respond to this question. Also, 53 percent of clinical psychologists believed that having religious beliefs was desirable for individuals in general, 33 percent were neutral, and 14 percent believed that having religious beliefs was undesirable. Fifty-one percent of the respondents described their spiritual practices and beliefs as an "alternative spiritual path which is not a part of organized religion," and 18 percent noted organized religion as their primary source of spirituality (p. 74). Moreover, 74 percent of the participants did not agree with the statement that "religious or spiritual issues are outside the scope of psychology" (p. 75).

In a later replication of this study, Shafranske (1995) surveyed 253 psychologists who were randomly selected from a listing of APA members in either Counseling Psychology (Division 17) or Clinical Psychology (Division 12). The results of this study were similar to those found in the previously mentioned study (Shafranske and Maloney, 1990). For example, 37.5 percent of the psychologists supported a "personal, transcendent God" orientation; 37.9 percent a "transcendent dimension exists in all nature" orientation; 23.5 percent an "all ideologies are illusions yet meaningful" orientation; and 1.2 percent an "all ideologies are illusions and irrelevant to the world" orientation. Also, 50 percent of the respondents described their spiritual practices and beliefs as an alternative path that is not a part of organized religion, and 16 percent noted organized religion as their primary source of spirituality.

Other Studies

These findings were consistent with the results of other studies (Kelly, 1995; Lannert, 1992). Lannert (1992) found that 50 percent of the internship training directors who responded to a survey viewed their personal spirituality as relevant yet independent from organized religion. Kelly (1995) surveyed 479 counselors randomly selected from the 1993 American Counseling Association's membership list. The results of this study indicated that "almost 90 percent of the counselor respondents indicated some degree of spiritual or religious orientation" (p. 652). Although approximately 70 percent of these counselors reported an affiliation with an organized religion, spiritual values were once again more widely professed than were religious values (Kelly, 1995).

The results of these more recent studies suggest that many mental health professionals viewed spiritual and religious beliefs as an important aspect of their lives. However, one can clearly see that the majority of therapists indicate a consistent preference for spiritual over religious values. This distinction, although it may seem minor, has very important implications for theory and practice, both inside and outside the therapy room. The findings of these studies beg the question, "Do the beliefs of therapists actually influence the behavior of therapists?"

Self-Reflexercise

Imagine for a moment that you wake up one morning on a day off from work, feeling well-rested. You get out of bed and go into your kitchen. Perhaps you turn on the coffeemaker or reach in the refrigerator for your favorite morning beverage. Then you walk to the front door, open it, and go outside to get the morning paper. You come back inside, sit down in your favorite chair, and read the paper.

Which section of the paper would you read first? Why? Which section of the paper would you read next? Why? Which section(s) of the paper would you likely never read? Why?

We ask you these questions to normalize the reality that people typically pay more attention to the things in life that interest them more than they do the things in life that interest them less. In turn, therapists pay more attention to the topics, words, and issues that interest them more. Again, we make no claim that this is rocket science. Yet we wonder why so many people in our field deny this to be the case for the therapist inside the therapy room. Personally, we believe this is a number one in geometry proofs. It's a given. As therapists, we constantly attend to certain things that clients say and marginalize others. This does not mean that we are inattentive or bad therapists. It simply means that we are human. It is impossible to attend to everything. Therefore, it's important for therapists to examine themselves to discover which issues and/or words they are most likely to prioritize.

For those who would suggest that our theory is without foundation, this reality has been demonstrated in empirical research (Shafranske and Malony, 1990; Kahle, 1997; Demling, Woerthmueller, and O'Connolly, 2001). Shafranske and Malony (1990) discovered that *both the attitudes and behaviors of therapists were primarily influenced by their personal view of religion and spirituality.* The more negatively the psychologist viewed his or her religious experiences in the past, the less likely he or she was to use explicit interventions of a religious nature. Consequently, the more positively the psychologist viewed his or her religious experiences in the past, the more likely he or she was to use interventions of a religious nature. In addition, religious participation and affiliation were positively related to the psychologist's use of explicit interventions of a religious nature in the past. In our study, *the religious orientation of therapists was related to their willingness to both explicitly and implicitly integrate spirituality and psychotherapy.* Not surprisingly, marriage and family therapists were significantly more willing to explicitly integrate both spirituality and God and therapy than were psychologists. Demling, Woerthmueller, and O'Connolly (2001) found *a correlation between the attitude of therapists toward religion and their handling of the issue in therapeutic practice.*

We believe that therapists' own values, preferences, and beliefs greatly influence what they attend to in therapy, and that professors' own values, preferences, and beliefs very much influence what they address in their classes. Again, this doesn't necessarily make these individuals inattentive or bad professors. It simply affirms them as human professors. However, if this were denied, perhaps we would question the competence of such a professor. There are few things worse in the therapeutic fields than a professor who has little clue about his or her own issues teaching others how to be aware of their own issues in therapy.

REAL-LIFE IMPLICATIONS

Recall the story of Susan, which we titled Supervising with a Back-Pew Driver. Susan sought guidance for working with a client who was a Christian. Her instructor's own beliefs about religion influenced how she chose to address the issue of religious beliefs in training. The professor acknowledged that she had little specific knowledge of the Christian faith and subsequently deferred to another student, who claimed to be a Christian, to offer advice to Susan. In our opinion, a poor process was utilized and poor advice was given. Why? Because the resulting advice was to have Susan go and impose another person's spiritual views onto the client, assuming that because they both identified with the Christian label this intervention would be consistent with the client's value and belief system. How did that ninth-grade physical science teacher explain "assume" again?

We make no claim that there is one right way to address spirituality in therapy. In fact, we would argue against such a claim. However, we do believe that there are many wrong ways of addressing spirituality in therapy. We could probably spend two chapters critiquing the preceding example. However, this example is not the problem; it simply illustrates the problem. The problem is that this type of incident happens all too often, in many different ways, shapes, and forms simply because many of the professors, therapists, and therapists in training are flying by the seats of their untrained pants. As a result, actions are taken in therapy based on uneducated guesses that are often based on nothing more than their own partially thought out personal values, beliefs, and opinions. In other words, attempts at value-free and value-neutral therapy inevitably result in a process where value-laden therapy unintentionally prevails.

However, many professionals appear to be clueless regarding this reality. In fact, somehow some people in the mental health field, upon hearing this assertion, seem more shocked than a confederate in a Milgram study. If you don't believe us, try throwing out this assertion by Martin Luther in a professional forum.

> The way of the world is such that people cannot bear the truth. (Luther, 1959, p. 1399)

Rather than taking the time to organize such a professional forum to prove our assertion, we thought it would be more effective to simply pose some additional questions based on our examination up to this point.

- Is it possible that professionals do not see this learned avoidance as a problem because it has been rationalized away as "good psychology" based on the opinions of some of the historical figures in psychology?
- Is it possible that many professors and training supervisors could unknowingly avoid addressing religious and spiritual issues proactively in training because of their own personal beliefs and/or discomfort related to religion and spirituality?
- Is it possible that this learned avoidance on the part of the instructors in the classroom could translate into learned avoidance on the part of therapists in the therapy room?
- Is it possible that practitioners have, at times, been enablers in this process because we have not spoken out loudly enough regarding the issues clients present in therapy?

Alan Jenkins, a gifted psychotherapist from Australia, wrote an excellent book titled *Invitations to Responsibility: The Therapeutic Engagement of Men Who Are Violent and Abusive* (1990). In this book, Jenkins highlights his work with men who abuse women and children. Jenkins masterfully offers men who have been abusive invitations to take responsibility for their actions. He doesn't beat them over the head with words such as "You must stop," nor does he ignore the issue due to his own discomfort in this area. Instead, Jenkins chooses other pathways to invite clients into honest processes of change through which they can accept responsibility for their actions. Both of us have watched Jenkins work in a clinical environment and have been impressed. Jenkins asks men who have a history of abusing their wives and/or their children questions such as, "When you abuse . . . I'm sorry. Is it OK to call it what it is?" We obviously don't need to explain the impact this type of question can have on a therapeutic process. However, we would like to briefly point out that Jenkins is able to deal with the tough issue in a way that invites others toward responsibility and change rather than pathologizing men who abuse. In fact, he invites these men to establish a mission in responsibility.

In a similar spirit, let's address the reality of where the mental health field is today with regard to the integration of spirituality and psychotherapy. Should we ignore clients' values and beliefs, being ignorant of the influence that our own values and beliefs have on the therapeutic process? Do we expect therapists in training to become aware of their own issues and either passively ignore or actively deny the existence of the pink elephants in the ivory tower? Do we support learned avoidance and contribute to myths such as, "discussing spirituality in therapy is unethical" and "discussing therapy will inevitably lead to an imposition of values" (ignorant of the fact that this myth is itself a value imposition)? Do we continue to settle for an overall failing grade in training? Oh, we're sorry. Is it OK to call it what it is?

The pink elephants are wearing no clothes! Believe us, it's not a pretty sight. Indeed, there is much work to do. We can and we must make healthy, perhaps difficult changes. And yet even in the face of the obstacles there is good news. The mental health care field has a history of resiliency, openness, honesty, and determination when it comes to doing what's in the best interest of clients and society in general. Rather than beating ourselves up and/or denying that the

Copyright Andrew Kendall. Used by permission.

problem is, indeed, very real, we hope that the mental health care field will collectively and individually choose to take an alternative pathway toward change. For neither denial nor beating ourselves up will lead us toward the healthy change that is needed. We need to establish a mission in responsibility.

This can be done effectively. After acknowledging the historical gap between clinicians and patients in the areas of spiritual and religious beliefs, the American Psychiatric Association demonstrated responsibility by taking official actions to ensure that competent training in these areas be established in training programs (Lu, 2000). In fact, seventy-two of the 125 undergraduate medical schools in the United States now have courses on how to effectively work with patients' spiritual concerns (Leach, 2000). Cheers to the American Psychiatric Association for demonstrating a strong commitment to face the pink elephants in the field and for choosing to support the needs of the majority of their patients in this important area of human diversity. Unfortunately, as previously discussed, research has not demonstrated the same type of response occurring in other mental health fields (Schulte, Skinner, and Claiborn, 2002).

Indeed, healthy change can occur from simply being consistent with the beliefs we espouse as a field. In fact, the mental health care field already has in place a process that can help us make positive, healthy changes that will benefit both clients and therapists. For after all, the field of psychotherapy is not that much different from the working field of one psychotherapist. Based on the empirical facts that most clients who enter our offices value spirituality and religion, and therapists report that clients often initiate such conversations, we suggest that the mental health care fields learn about themselves by learning from themselves. We strongly urge the mental health care fields to take part in a "systemic reflexive process"! In so doing, we, as collective fields, can become more aware of our own issues, values, assumptions, beliefs, and biases that have historically contributed to us not handling these issues in the healthiest, most honest way possible.

CONCLUSION

The time is always right to do what is right.

Martin Luther King Jr.

We are at a choice point. We can continue to choose to ignore and/or to deny. However, if we are to be an ethical field consistent with our own espoused beliefs, we must strive to obtain the training, experience, consultation, or supervision necessary to ensure the competence of their services, or make appropriate referrals. If we are to be an ethical field with regard to the integration of spirituality and psychotherapy, we have only given ourselves one option. Externalize it if you must, but we *must* address the God phobia, antireligious bias, and aspiritualism directly and strive to make healthy and ethical changes. For if we do not, *to whom shall we refer?*

If not us, who? If not now, when? It is ethical, it is desired, and it is time!

SECTION II: HOW THEN SHALL WE COUNSEL?

Without counsel purposes are disappointed: but in the multitude of counselors they are established.

King Solomon
Proverbs 15:22 (King James Version)

Chapter 9

To Believe or Not to Believe? That Is *Not* the Question!

The difficulties of belief may be great, but the problems inherent in unbelief present even greater difficulties.

Josh McDowell
More Than a Carpenter

Since Bergin (1980a) asserted that individuals implement their own values systems via their professional work, research has proven this to be the case time and time again (Bergin and Jensen, 1990; Shafranske and Malony, 1990; Kahle, 1997). We believe that individuals do implement their own values systems in their work, and we believe that this is *not* a problem in and of itself. However, this implementation of values systems is a problem if the therapist implements his or her values system without respecting the values system of the client or is either unaware of this process and/or denies that this is in fact the case. For the person of the therapist and the professional of the therapist are not any more mutually exclusive than are the person of the president and the professional of the president. So, rather than wasting time looking for some mythological switch to turn off, perhaps it would be best if we were to invest our time more wisely by searching for Bigfoot, the Loch Ness Monster, or perhaps we could simply embrace the fact that *therapists implement their own values systems every day they work.* Everything else we'll discuss related to the integration of spirituality, religion, and psychotherapy hinges on this belief about belief! Since we both embrace the fact that the person and the professional of the therapist are not mutually exclusive entities, perhaps a brief summary of our values orientations would be important in explaining how we conceptualize spirituality in our personal and professional lives.

TRUTH, JUSTICE, AND A THERAPEUTIC WAY

We are both Christians. I (Peter) am a Lutheran and John is a Catholic. In other words, we're simply a Reformation apart. Although we're both Christians, we don't agree on everything within the realms of spirituality and religion. We both believe that the Triune God is our spiritual source, our maker, our comforter, our hope, and our God. Therefore, we strongly embrace the belief that a person's spiritual faith in God can be a powerful source of help and healing in his or her life. However, we also understand that certain beliefs about God can be a powerful hindrance in a person's life, sometimes creating a barrier that prevents individuals from experiencing healthy, balanced lives. Since we hold these beliefs to be true outside of therapy, it should come as no surprise that we hold these beliefs to be true inside of the therapeutic environment as well. Therefore, we approach the topic of spirituality in therapy in an intelligently cautious manner. We stand in reverence of power.

Since addressing the subject of spirituality in therapy involves more than just spiritual values, it may also be helpful for us to briefly summarize our values orientations related to "belief" and "truth." On more than one occasion, we have seen a therapist's fear of talking about his or her truth orientation unintentionally contribute to avoidance of spiritual issues in therapy, even God phobia at times. We strongly believe that each and every therapist has beliefs, issues, and biases that can, and will, influence the therapeutic process. Therefore, we use the term *belief* intentionally.

We are aware that many of the popular theorists of today, particularly postmodern theorists, make use of the term *assumption* when speaking of the personal beliefs that guide them in the therapeutic process. We've heard a number of these colleagues explain that by using the term *assumption,* they experience greater freedom and flexibility in therapy because they are not as wed to a particular belief, position, or stance. Although we trust that their hearts may be in good places, we respectfully challenge the assumption that believing in something strongly necessarily leads to less freedom and/or decreased flexibility in therapy.

There are important distinctions between beliefs and assumptions. Assumption is defined by Webster's (1984) as "(a) something taken to be true without proof or demonstration, (b) presumption or arrogance, (c) a minor premise." Webster's defines belief as "(a) the mental act, condition, or habit of placing trust or confidence in a person or thing, (b) mental acceptance of or conviction in the truth or actuality of something." We don't want the very things on which we build our theoretical foundation to be "minor premises" or to assume something to be true without any proof or demonstration.

Of course, we understand that our postmodern colleagues, constructivists, social constructionists, and deconstructionists alike, also intentionally choose the words they use. (*Note:* We are fully aware that those who identify themselves with one of these theoretical labels will undoubtedly disagree with the lumping together of the various schools of thought into the term *postmodernists.* However, we make no claim that this is an exhaustive critique of various theoretical positions underneath the postmodern umbrella. Hence, the grouping is intended and subsequent objections are noted, understood, and marginalized for the purpose of this very brief discussion.) Postmodernists likely prefer assumption to belief because they would explain that mental acceptance of or conviction in the truth or actuality of something is a modernistic way of thinking. They would likely even smile at our use of Webster's dictionary, questioning our modernistic assumption that a book could actually contain the true definition of a word. Of course, we are then left to wonder why these masters of parenthetical discourse do not pick up on their own modernistic assumption that a book could not contain a true definition of a word. Regardless, from a postmodern perspective, truth is viewed as a subjective, internally constructed or socially constructed reality that results in the creation of multiple truths and multiple realities. Consequently, they believe that there is no such thing as absolute truth (or "Capital T," as they often refer to it).

Let us be very clear here. We love our postmodern colleagues and greatly respect their work related to challenging practitioners to think, in great depth, about epistemological and ontological issues. We simply believe that they, too, could benefit from some self-reflexivity related to the postulates they hold. C. S. Lewis ([1943] 1996) astutely asserted,

> The scientist has to assume the validity of his own logic (in the stout old fashion of Plato or Spinoza) even in order to prove that it is merely subjective, and therefore he can only flirt with subjectivism. (p. 223)

A belief that there is no such thing as absolute truth is self-contradictory. For if the statement is true, the statement has proven itself to be false. This is a statement that is predicated on the foundation of absolute truth. Furthermore, if a person believes in the concept that there is no true reality, but rather only multiple realities, a person must be open to the possibility that one of those multiple realities could be the existence of an absolute reality. We use the term must intentionally, not based on our espoused belief system, but rather based on the belief system espoused by persons who hold this belief. Hence, a person who believes only in multiple realities must believe that absolute reality is a possibility if he or she is to remain consistent with his or her own stated beliefs. Of course a person does not have to be open to this possibility. He or she simply has to be open to this possibility if he or she chooses to avoid the suicide of thought. G. K. Chesterton ([1936] 1966) asserted,

> But when people begin to talk about universal relativity, as if everything were as relative as everything else, so that presumably the very notion of relativity is itself relative, only relative to nobody knows what, they are simply knocking the bottom out of the world and the human brain, and leaving a bottomless abyss of bosh. (p. 141)

All human beings believe. Although they choose what they believe, they do not have a choice in whether or not they believe. To be human is to believe. As a popular rock group of the 1980s, Rush, asserted in one of their songs, "If you decide not to decide, you still have made a choice." Furthermore, we'll even go as far as to contend that every human being believes in some form of absolute truth. For example, in the spiritual realm, the spiritual relativist who believes that every spiritual tradition simply uses different metaphors to worship the same deity is no less an absolutist than is the Christian who believes that faith in Jesus Christ as one's Savior is the only way to Heaven. Although these two people differ at the content level, at the process level they are both very much professing a belief in absolute truth. This holds true for atheists and others as well. Yes, even agnostics; for isn't the self-professing agnostic certain of his or her uncertainty?

We are fully aware that there are many people who would disagree with us on this point. In fact, make this assertion in many professional

Copyright Andrew Kendall. Used by permission.

settings and you're likely to feel about as comfortable as Salman Rushdie at a Khomeini family reunion. However, we welcome this disagreement for we understand that to simply believe that there is no absolute truth does not make it so. This belief simply demonstrates that those who hold this belief absolutely believe in the truth that we are wrong on this point. In our opinion, to believe that a person does not believe does not demonstrate superior intellectual wisdom, but rather simply demonstrates an ignorance of the fact that this is a blind spot for the person who holds this belief. Let's move beyond truth by realizing that we can never move beyond Truth.

> *All roads lead to Rome; which is one reason why many people never get there.*
>
> G. K. Chesterton
> *Orthodoxy*

Peter Senge and his colleagues (1994) use an excellent drawing of a mental model of cognitive thought processing (Figure 9.1) in their

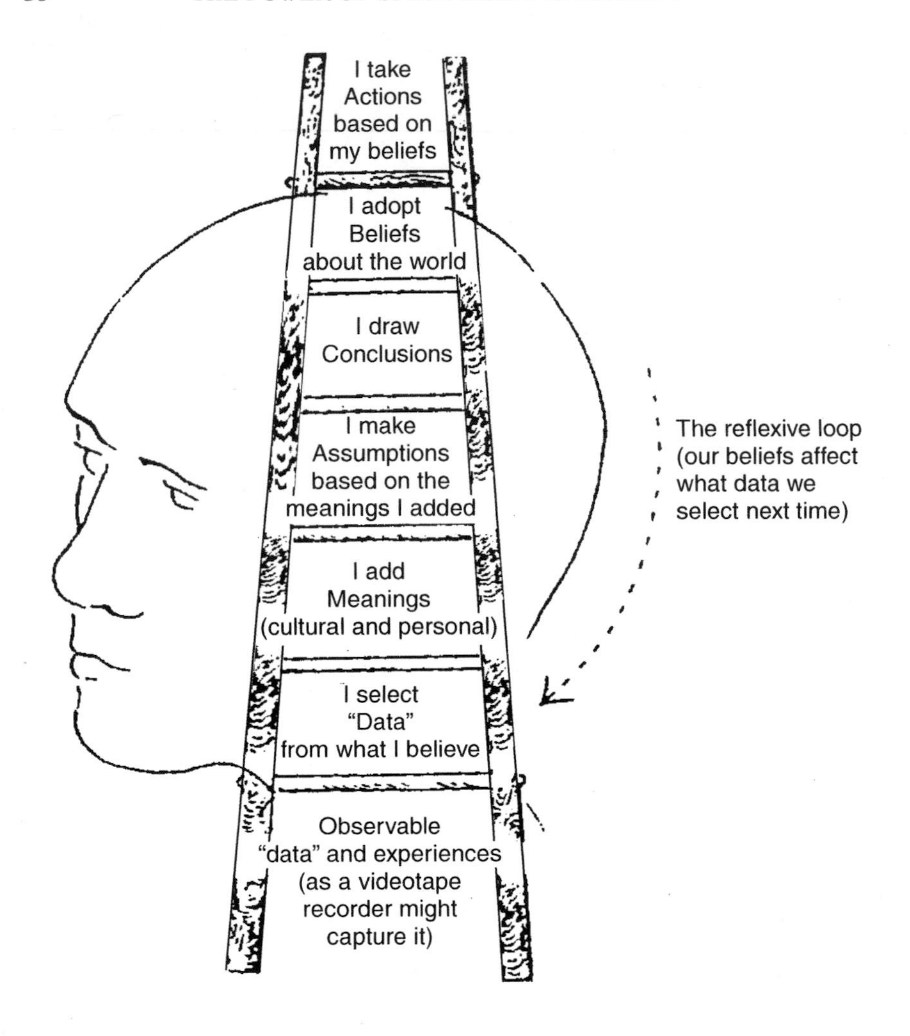

FIGURE 9.1. The ladder of inference, a model of cognitive processing. (*Source:* Senge et al., 1994, p. 243)

book to help illustrate the fact that assumptions and beliefs are different, but important, parts in a ladder of inference. Their illustration reaffirms the importance of increasing our awareness of the influence that both assumptions and beliefs can have on thought processes and behavior. Therapists who believe they do not believe and/or do not understand the process of a reflexive loop will undoubtedly experience difficulties inside and outside the therapy room.

We've heard several people assert that they do not have beliefs about spirituality. Some have suggested, "I reject all spiritual belief systems." If a person chooses to reject all spiritual belief systems, that is fine with us. However, we refuse to enter into a collusion of ignorance if the person asserts that he or she "therefore does not hold any beliefs about spirituality." For, to reject all spiritual belief systems is to hold a belief system about spirituality.

Denial of beliefs about spirituality is common in the mental health fields today. We can't tell you how many times we've heard a colleague assert that he or she does not hold beliefs about spirituality, but then follow this statement with an aspiritualistic diatribe that makes it very clear that he or she thinks spirituality is a crutch for the weak and cognitively limited. We've seen this blind spot contribute to problems in the therapeutic process when these therapists work with people for whom spirituality is an important aspect of their lives. We refer to this problematic process as the "entrapment of not owning." If a therapist does not own and/or is not aware of his or her beliefs about spirituality, the beliefs will eventually own the therapist and the client, and subsequently become a hindrance in the therapeutic process.

Rather than try to achieve the impossible in becoming free of values in therapy, we embrace our beliefs in an attempt to increase our awareness of how our beliefs can potentially impact the therapeutic process. In the hit movie *The Hunt for Red October* (1990), Sean Connery plays the role of a Russian submarine commander, Captain Marko Ramius. In one memorable scene, he instructs the crew to turn the submarine around and speed directly into the oncoming path of two torpedoes that were fired from an enemy submarine. Obviously, many of the crew think Captain Ramius is making a reckless decision that will certainly end the lives of everyone aboard the submarine. However, by turning the sub completely around and speeding directly into the path of the potential danger, the sub is able to close the distance gap and make contact with the torpedoes before they are able to arm themselves, thus destroying the torpedoes. In so doing, rather than ignoring the danger or trying to outrun that which they could not outrun, or dodge that which they could not dodge, they are able to eliminate destruction by embracing the potential for danger, thus eliminating the destructive force of the torpedoes.

This is an example of recognizing and embracing our potential limitations rather than ignoring and/or denying that they exist. This is recognizing the paradox rather than being controlled by it. This is trying to control what we can control and giving up trying to control what we can't, and recognizing the difference between the two. This is what we call "ceasing to headbutt the Serenity Prayer." This is a pathway to freedom. Indeed, as you will soon discover, research suggests that this type of approach may better help therapists work with their clients' spiritual beliefs than does trying to achieve the mythical value-free or value-neutral posture in therapy.

To believe or not to believe is not the question. In the end, every therapist needs to confront the reality that "I believe." Therefore, the more operative questions appear to be, "In what do I believe, and how will my beliefs impact the counseling process?"

FIVE OF OUR THERAPEUTIC BELIEFS

We believe you deserve to know our beliefs, especially because we expect that you may not agree with everything we assert. We hope you will understand that this disagreement is perfectly fine with us. We have no problem with disagreement. In fact, we believe that honest and loving disagreement is healthy at times. Rather than encourage you to see the world as we do, we simply encourage you to open yourself up to the possibility of seeing things in ways that may be new and unique to you.

Before specifically going into a discussion about our beliefs related to the integration of spirituality and therapy, we think it would be helpful to articulate five of our central beliefs about the therapeutic process in general. Regardless of whether or not we're addressing spiritual issues in therapy, we hold these beliefs to be central to the manner in which we practice. We're placing these beliefs on top of the table, because we believe that they provide the foundation for why we are willing to, and how we do, address spiritual issues in therapy. Indeed, the person of the therapist is not mutually exclusive with the professional of the therapist when addressing spiritual issues in therapy.

1. Individuals, couples, and families have stories of competence that have been marginalized (White, 1986).

> *Every story one chooses to tell is a kind of censorship: it prevents the telling of other tales.*
>
> Salman Rushdie
> *Shame*

We believe that every human being has strengths and competencies . . . dare we say, "God-given gifts"? I (Peter) used the terminology one time in my graduate training and one of my professors challenged me on this by asking, "What about people who do not believe in God? Do they have God-given gifts as well?" We would simply respond from our belief system that God is an equal opportunity gift giver. We believe that God does not withhold gifts from people based on what human beings do or do not do. Indeed, some people have been given certain gifts that others do not have. What human beings do with these gifts (e.g., their talents) is a different matter altogether.

However, although we believe that every human being possesses certain gifts, strengths, and competencies, we also believe that human beings sometimes struggle with recognizing them. In fact, many people are much more adept at recognizing their weaknesses and/or shortcomings than they are their strengths and talents. Ask a person to list his or her weaknesses and you will often hear a long list of things the individual believes he or she does not do well. However, ask the same person to tell you about his or her strengths and/or what he or she is good at, and you will likely hear more silence and a much shorter list, if you hear a list at all.

Since we believe that every human being has strengths, and that people typically have a difficult time recognizing their own strengths, we believe that one of our responsibilities as therapists is to encourage our clients to explore the possibility that they have marginalized stories of competence in their own lives. One of the ways that we make this point is in the form of an easy-to-understand example. Just as you, the reader, were not consciously aware of the pressure on your buttocks from the chair in which you are now sitting (or from the bed in which you are lying) until we brought it to your attention, make no mistake, the pressure did, indeed, exist before your attention was drawn to it. The simple fact is that we are not able to attend to everything we're experiencing at a given point in time. Similarly, we walk through life paying attention to certain things that happen to us and not paying attention to other things that happen to us.

Many of our clients come into therapy with problem-saturated stories. However, if we pay close attention to their stories, we'll also be able to hear stories of strengths and competencies. We're aware that the client's problem-saturated perspective often prevents him or her from seeing these stories of strength and competence. This presents both an opportunity and a challenge to the therapist. The competent therapist would be wise to avoid attempting to convince the client that everything going on in his or her life is rosy and that everything would be better if he or she were to simply change his or her perspective. However, we believe that it's also counterproductive to hold a problem-saturated perspective toward our clients' stories as we would likely try to develop a problem-saturated intervention to help them. Yet we are aware that the isomorphic reality of this process is very common in psychotherapy. Therefore, we try to help our clients see their own stories of competence over time by simply inviting them, through the art of questioning, to attend to the parts of their own stories in which competencies and strengths are clearly visible.

2. Competence should be thought of in a systemic framework for therapy.

In recent years, competency-focused therapies have increased in popularity. (We certainly claim no original thought with regard to the above discussion on the marginalization of competence in clients' life stories.) Indeed, they have helped therapists develop new perspectives to help clients escape the grasp of unhealthy problem-saturated stories in their lives. However, we have witnessed a new phenomenon in some competency-focused circles we refer to as "competency-saturation therapy." In a desire to help clients see their strengths and competencies, we must be careful not to lead our clients to the other extreme of the continuum, an unrealistic, competency-saturated view of life. Before we use an example to further illustrate this point, consider the following question: *When is it incompetent on the part of a therapist to focus on a client's competence?*

We observed a training exercise a few years ago in which a reflecting team was being used in the therapeutic process with a family that was trying to confront their teenage son's unhealthy behavior. His father had told a story in which his son had been in trouble with the law and had refused to listen to his father. During the session, we observed the son laughing as his father told a story in which his son had recently stolen his ATM card out of his wallet and had used it to get money to purchase cocaine for him and his friends. The father appeared to have a sense of helplessness as he looked down and said that he didn't know what to do. The therapist in the room asked the son a question about his cocaine use and the son confirmed that he indeed was using cocaine, enjoyed it, and did not think that he had a problem. Shortly after he had mentioned that he was failing most of his classes due to skipping school and doing drugs with his friends during school hours, he commented that he wanted to become a doctor. We must admit at this point that we don't remember the exact words that were used by the therapist in the room, but the next question the therapist posed to the teenager was something similar to, "Well, you're obviously good at some things. Tell me about how you are able to balance the cocaine on your finger before you snort it."

Sometimes, one can fall into the trap of what we call "the social construction of competence." Involved in a difficult search to find a strength and competency of the client, the therapist can, unintentionally, attempt to create a client's competency. Unfortunately, this did not go over very well with the client's father and some valuable time was spent backtracking and trying to repair the damaged therapeutic bridge. This, of course, is not a potential problem that only resides within the competency-based therapies. If devotion to a particular mindset outweighs devotion to common sense, any theory has the potential to lead the therapist toward therapeutic incompetence.

It's important for therapists to think reflexively to make sure that they are primarily aware of their own competencies and ideas about competent therapeutic work before focusing on discovering their clients' strengths and competencies. We believe the therapeutic goal should be one of systemic competence. Otherwise, there's a greater risk for the therapist to participate in the social construction of competence and/or competency-saturated therapy, both of which we contend would more likely lead the therapist and client toward the incompetent end of the therapeutic continuum of competence.

3. Solutions and successes are often best constructed in terms of the presence of something, rather than the absence of something.

Michael White (1989) gave the therapeutic community an excellent gift when he explained the therapeutic technique he labeled "externalizing the problem" in great depth. White demonstrated that excellent therapeutic gain can result from externalizing the problem, thereby inviting families to rally around each other, working together toward healthy problem resolution and helping them to avoid the trap of equating the person with the problem. In these instances, therapeutic success is defined in relation to the problem.

We suggest (Kahle and Robbins, 1999a,b) that White's general ideas could also be applied to a therapeutic technique we refer to as "externalizing the success." Sometimes, individuals and families are making excellent therapeutic progress, yet have a difficult time internalizing personal agency for these positive changes. Some clients may find it difficult to see that they have played an integral role in making positive changes in their lives. They may attribute the change to things such as the weather, luck, or simply say, "It just happened." In cases such as these, it's sometimes helpful to externalize the client's defined goals and/or success to help him or her explore the possibility that he or she has actually played an integral role in achieving the desired changes in his or her life. In these instances, therapeutic success is defined in regard to the achieved success, not the problem.

For example, we worked with a family who had entered therapy to work on improving communication. During the course of therapy, we discovered that there was a great deal of anger within this family. The anger often prevented family members from clearly articulating what it was they expected from one another and prevented them from hearing those family members who were able to articulate their expectations. This family responded very well to externalizing the problem, so we spent several sessions mapping and tracking the influence of "anger" in the life of the family. When they started to make positive changes in their lives, the family members struggled to see how they had played a part in pushing the anger away from their family. In response to the question, "What's going on differently in the home now that anger isn't around as much?" the youngest boy commented that it was cool. We started to unpack the client's perception of what "cool" was, and soon discovered that "coolness" was very much different than simply the absence of the problem. The family members all agreed that the "coolness" was great and responded well to our questions about the "coolness." Before long, we invited the family members into a process where they explored and gained insight into what they had done and could continue to do to invite more coolness into their lives.

In other counseling scenarios, we have seen some excellent therapeutic gains occur in the lives of individuals, couples, and families, whom we have helped to learn how to simply "grow the good" in their lives rather than trying to "shrink the bad." We've found that these therapeutic approaches can often complement each other quite well. This has also been helpful as we've invited our supervisees into discussions that have challenged their erroneous assumption that therapy is over when problem resolution occurs. After all, many clients are presented with new challenges when problem resolution occurs, such as "What do I do with all of my time now? What's next? Maybe it was better the old way?" Indeed, reflexivity need not stop when resolution seems to have occurred with regard to the client's presenting problem.

4. It's impossible to work without a box! However, unpacking our own beliefs and values can open space for maneuverability within a box.

We have all heard the phrase, "Thinking outside of the box." Although we appreciate the usefulness that can result from encouraging people to think in new ways or see something new as a result of taking a different perspective, we believe that this can be taken too far. *We believe that human beings are always thinking within a box. As soon as human beings think that they are thinking outside the box, they have simply demonstrated that they have entered a new one.*

We had to laugh one day as we listened to two of our colleagues disagreeing with each other. Each was trying to show the other that he was not seeing things clearly because he was not thinking outside of the box. They were both trying to convince each other that they were thinking outside of the box. Both individuals were totally unaware of what was occurring at a process level. They were both thinking in a box!

We use the concept of a habitrail as an analogy for the healthy self-reflexive habits of a therapist. The habitrail is the combination of tubes, containers, and other devices that make up the caged home for some hamsters and gerbils. The animals can enter into new areas and experience new freedom from possible isolation through choosing different pathways. As a result of thinking in different ways, the animals can find sources of food, drink, comfort, and means of exercising that are unavailable to them if they were to remain in the same place. However, the animals cannot leave the habitrail itself without the help of their owners. Although we claim no working knowledge of the psychological and intellectual functioning of rodents, we would hypothesize that the animals who enjoy the freedom within the limitations of the habitrail are more content than those who sit in one area of the habitrail, frustrated that they cannot escape the confines of the habitrail.

What one individual may see as limiting, another may see as freeing. With that in mind, what a therapist may believe to be limiting could prove to be freeing. Of course, the reverse could also be true. What a therapist may believe to be freeing could prove to be limiting. The same logic holds true for clients as well.

> There is no completely open conversational space in therapy just as there is no totally neutral therapist. Therapist and client are always opening and closing doors to new places together, looking for that which has not been seen, listening for that which has not been heard, negotiating together the limits and the possibilities. (Griffith, 1995b, pp. 123-124)

5. Value-free therapy is a myth/an impossibility (Bergin, 1980a).

We believe it's impossible for a therapist to be value-free. *To be human is to value.* Thus, it's impossible for a cognitively alert human being to cease valuing. A person can most certainly try, but in so doing, he or she is actually placing a great value on getting rid of his or her values.

In saying this, we also reject the idea of value neutrality. We believe that value-neutral therapy is also a myth. Even though Carl Rogers, as early as 1957, admitted that a therapist could not practice without supplying evidence of personal values and views of human nature, and Jensen and Bergin (1988) demonstrated empirically that value-free and value-neutral therapy are myths, we believe these myths are still very alive today.

A TV commercial about a toy that was popular back in the 1980s, Transformers, had a jingle that went something similar to, "Transformers, robots in disguise." This line of toys could quickly be turned from a robot into other objects, such as a racecar. Although the one object could change into another, the parts making up the other object were still very present. We see a similarity between these toys and the ideas of value-free therapy.

When it became relatively accepted that value-free therapy was impossible, the term value-neutral therapy became more prevalent. Now that it has become more accepted that value-neutral therapy is impossible, we believe that these notions have been transformed into another term that is popular in our society and the mental health field today. Indeed, although empirically proven to be dead, the myths of value-free and value-neutral therapy have been transformed and are very alive today under the identity of open-mindedness. C. S. Lewis ([1947] 1996) said, "For what we call 'primitive errors' do not pass away. They merely change their form" (p. 74). We will address this assertion in great detail in upcoming chapters.

These five beliefs about the therapeutic process have helped form our foundation for striving to become more competent therapists in the art of integrating spirituality, religion, and psychotherapy.

Chapter 10

The Integration of Religion, Spirituality, and Clinical Practice

Psychotherapists are the socially sanctioned protectors of hope.

Michael Mahoney
"Self-Care for the Psychotherapists"

IS INTEGRATION DESIRED?

Taking into account the high percentage of religious people in society, clinical practitioners, even those who are not religious themselves, are likely to encounter a number of religious clients and issues. Although most clinical practitioners reported that they believed religious issues were relevant to clinical practice, the majority of these clinicians acknowledged that psychologists do not generally have the skills or knowledge base to help individuals with regard to spiritual or religious issues (Shafranske and Malony, 1990). This situation may be problematic at times, since religious clients may want religious issues to be incorporated into therapy (Quackenbos, Privette, and Klentz, 1985). Many clinicians have undoubtedly felt more helpless than a dog in a Seligman study. However, rather than simply assuming and/or theorizing that some clients may want spiritual or religious issues incorporated into therapy, let's put the question on the table: Is there a demand for the integration of spirituality, religion, and psychotherapy?

1. A 1993 Gallup (Gallup Poll Monthly, 1993) study found that 66 percent of surveyed Americans indicated they would prefer a counselor who was religious.

2. In a study published in the *Journal of Counseling Psychology,* Rose, Westefeld, and Ansely (2001) found clients believed that discussions about religious concerns were appropriate for counseling and had a preference for discussing religious and spiritual issues in therapy. These researchers noted that spiritual experience was the most powerful explanatory variable for preferences related to discussing spiritual/religious issues.
3. Another study, conducted by Claudia Goedde (2001), also found that psychotherapy clients who believe that religion and/or spirituality are an important and integral part of their life appreciate a psychotherapeutic approach that is respectful, sensitive, and welcoming to their spiritual orientation. This researcher noted that the clients who participated in her study viewed the psychological and spiritual as deeply interconnected.

Based on empirical evidence, the answer to this question appears to be a resounding "Yes!" Since many clients indicate that they would like spiritual and/or religious issues integrated into therapy, let's shift our focus to address various approaches related to how therapists can address spiritual and/or religious issues in therapy.

Bergin, Payne, and Richards (1996) insisted that even if a therapist does not initiate an assessment of religious and spiritual needs, he or she should be open to such topics. These researchers assert "avoiding religious issues or routinely redirecting spiritual concerns in therapy is no more justifiable than refusing to deal with the death of a family member or fears of social encounters" (p. 313). Considering the history of debate within the field, it's no surprise to discover that unanimity has not existed within the field with regard to how religious and/or spiritual issues should be integrated into therapy.

EXPLICIT INTEGRATION

Tan (1996) describes the explicit integration of religion, spirituality, and psychotherapy as an "overt approach that directly and systematically deals with spiritual or religious issues in therapy and uses spiritual resources like prayer, scripture or sacred texts, referrals to church or religious groups or lay counselors, and other religious practices" (p. 368). Therapists who practice from an explicit integration model are usually, but not always, religious themselves, and are comfortable praying with clients aloud in therapy when appropriate (Tan, 1996). Religious clients, particularly those who are Christian, seemed to prefer more religiously oriented therapy that included the use of prayer and scripture, reporting that they found the use of prayer and scripture to be helpful (Tan, 1987, 1993).

Worthington and colleagues (1988) surveyed Christian mental health professionals and counselors and discovered that the most commonly used spiritual guidance techniques in therapy were assigning religious homework, quoting scripture, interpreting scripture, discussing the client's faith, and prayer. Moon and colleagues (1993) surveyed Christian psychotherapists, pastoral counselors, and spiritual directors to examine the use of Christian spiritual guidance techniques. They found that the surveyed psychotherapists and pastoral counselors most commonly used spiritual history, insight, forgiveness, silence, intercessory prayer, and teaching based on scripture. These researchers also found that master's-level practitioners were more likely to use these explicit methods than were doctoral-level practitioners. Others have explicitly integrated spiritual issues and therapy (Propst et al., 1992; Titone, 1996).

Peck (1993) suggested that a spiritual history should be routinely taken in much the same way that a general history and mental status exam are employed. Titone (1996) developed a comprehensive question checklist that is used to assess a client's spiritual life and suggests that "the spiritual component of an evaluation for psychotherapeutic purposes may be as important as any other component" (p. 25).

Shafranske and Malony (1990) discovered that many clinical psychologists were unwilling to use explicit religious interventions in therapy. They found that whether a psychologist had employed explicit methods in the past depended on how explicitly religious and participatory the psychologist perceived the intervention to be. For example, 57 percent of the surveyed psychologists had used religious language with a client, 36 percent had recommended participation in a religion, 32 percent had used or recommended religious or spiritual books, and only 7 percent had explicitly prayed with a client.

In addition to their reported behaviors, these researchers also surveyed the beliefs of the psychologists. They found that 68 percent of those surveyed believed it was inappropriate for psychologists to pray with clients, and 55 percent believed it was inappropriate to use religious texts in therapy. Of note was the finding that both the attitudes and behaviors of therapists were primarily influenced by their personal view of religion and spirituality (Shafranske and Malony, 1990). The more negatively the psychologist viewed his or her religious experiences in the past, the less likely he or she was to use explicit interventions of a religious nature. Conversely, the more positively the psychologist viewed his or her religious experiences in the past, the more likely he or she was to use interventions of a religious nature. In addition, religious participation and affiliation were positively related to the psychologist's use of explicit religious interventions in the past. Approximately 33 percent of the psychologists reported being personally competent in counseling clients regarding religious and spiritual issues. Thus, the religious beliefs and affiliations of these psychologists influenced the extent to which they were willing to explicitly integrate religious issues and psychotherapy.

In summary, both the attitudes and behaviors of psychologists were significantly influenced by their personal views about religion (Shafranske and Malony, 1990). Perhaps these empirical findings help give insight into why only 29 percent of the therapists surveyed viewed religious matters as important in the treatment of all or many of their clients (Bergin and Jensen, 1990).

Although there are some clear benefits of using an explicit integration model with religious clients, the explicit integration of religion, spirituality, and therapy can also create difficulties for the participants (Rotz, Russel, and Wright, 1993). Tan (1996) acknowledged that explicit approaches can potentially be misused by unethical therapists. Therefore, he states, "Explicit integration of religion in clinical practice should be practiced in a clinically sensitive, ethically responsible, and professionally competent way" (p. 369). Since explicitly integrating religion, spirituality, and psychotherapy can also create barriers that are detrimental to the therapeutic process, some practitioners may be more comfortable using nonexplicit means to integrate religion and psychotherapy. In fact, our research demonstrated that therapists are more willing to implicitly integrate, rather than explicitly integrate, spirituality, God, and psychotherapy (Kahle, 1997). Tan (1996) suggested that implicit means can also be used to integrate religious and/or spiritual issues in clinical practice in ethically responsible and competent ways.

IMPLICIT INTEGRATION

Tan (1996) describes the implicit integration of religion and clinical practice as "a more covert approach that does not initiate the discussion of religious or spiritual issues and does not openly, directly, or systematically use spiritual resources like prayer and Scripture or other sacred texts in therapy" (p. 368). In this model, religious issues are addressed if they are brought up by the client but the therapist does not initiate such conversation. Therapists who practice from an implicit model demonstrate respect for the religious beliefs of their clients, and maintain their own beliefs about religion. A therapist who practices from this approach could still be a religious person, but would not explicitly pray with his or her clients.

Therapists who utilize more implicit approaches to address religious and/or spiritual issues in therapy usually attempt to understand the religious beliefs of each individual client by focusing on the language the client uses to describe his or her religious beliefs and practices (Griffith and Griffith, 1992). Bergin, Payne, and Richards (1996) state:

> Experiencing empathy for clients, knowing something of their struggle and identifying with their dilemmas, depends on comprehending their beliefs, their moral framework, and their assumptive world. This understanding is approximated by being open to the client's perceptions and taking the position of being informed by the client. (p. 301)

Therefore, a therapist using an implicit approach must learn about each client's unique perceptions and spiritual and/or religious beliefs to be helpful to the religious and/or spiritual client.

Wulff (1996) suggested that a therapist who takes a relativistic stance toward religious expression allows each client the opportunity to describe his or her personal relationship with God. Stander and colleagues (1994) suggest:

> The religiously sensitive therapist must have the utmost respect for the ethic of religious autonomy. The client has the right to decide to hold whatever religious beliefs he or she wishes.

> Clearly, when the clients' decisions violate the rights of others or the clients are of questionable psychological competence, the ethic is in conflict, but most of the ongoing religious issues we confront are not this kind. (p. 31)

Thus, the ethic of religious autonomy allows the religiously sensitive therapist to respect the unique beliefs of each client without blindly supporting religious beliefs that are injurious.

Melissa Elliott and James Griffith have written extensively about the integration of spirituality in therapy (Griffith, 1986, 1995a, b,c; Griffith and Griffith, 1992). Griffith and Griffith (1992) suggest that every religious client has a God construct, which they described as "a mental construct existing as an autonomous cognitive structure. A God-construct is specific and unique for each individual" (p. 65). Griffith (1986) found that many families viewed God as a member of their family. He suggested that God, as an important family member, provided new therapeutic possibilities. He suggested that a therapist take a one-down position in therapy to allow the client to teach the therapist about God. Therefore, there is minimal risk of a therapeutic stalemate when the therapist and client conflict in their religious beliefs because the therapist works within the client's presented reality without providing a critique of that reality. He suggested that this approach opens space for the client to discuss his or her personal relationship with God with minimal risks.

These implicit approaches support the client and respectfully allow the client to discuss his or her unique personal conceptualization of God in therapy, if the client so chooses. This support and respect for religious autonomy can be useful, since some research has suggested that religious individuals were more likely to refer a Christian friend to a counselor who supported a client's religious beliefs than a counselor who challenged the religious beliefs of a client (McCullough and Worthington, 1995). Kudlac (1991) asserted that a therapist must be open to conversations about religious issues if he or she wishes to be helpful to religious clients who want to talk about religious issues. Also, we have previously asserted (Kahle and Robbins, 1998a,b) that encouraging a client to invite something he or she defines as beneficial into therapy may increase the likelihood for therapeutic success. Prest and Keller (1993) suggested that addressing spiritual issues in therapy can facilitate increased understanding of each client. Also, Kudlac (1991) states, "It is not necessary for the therapist to subscribe to the same beliefs held by the client; however, to be able to fully enter into a conversation, these beliefs must be addressed" (p. 281).

Tan (1996) suggested that explicit and implicit integration in clinical practice need not be considered mutually exclusive categories. He proposed that it may be more helpful to view these two concepts as the ends of an integration continuum, thus allowing a therapist to move to different points along the continuum depending on the problems and the needs of the client. Therefore, Tan (1996) suggested that a therapist may sometimes choose to explicitly introduce religious issues during therapy while, at other times, the therapist may follow the lead of the client who introduces religious issues. We agree with Tan that explicit and implicit integration in clinical practice are not necessarily mutually exclusive categories. We also believe that both can be helpful to the therapeutic process. Yet we were interested in learning more about some of the factors that help encourage therapists to integrate spirituality, religion, and psychotherapy in healthy and effective ways.

PATHWAYS TO INTEGRATION

Recall our discussion in Chapter 3 about the therapists' assumptions and/or beliefs that discouraged them from talking about God in therapy. We hoped that we could also gain insight into some of the factors that help to open pathways for sacred conversation to occur in therapy. With our loving apologies to Melissa Elliott, we wondered what type of information we could discover by addressing a slightly modified version of her previously mentioned question. Given that therapists, counselors, and clients want these conversations to occur, *what underlying assumptions and/or beliefs lead us to encourage them?* Once again, rather than simply assuming that therapists' assumptions and beliefs influence them in therapy, we posed an open-ended question to our respondents to see what assumptions and/or beliefs they believed influenced them in therapy. Participants were asked to respond to the question, "What assumptions and/or beliefs do you have that encouraged you to talk about God in therapy?" Three themes emerged from their responses (see Table 10.1). The following are some of the comments they used to describe their beliefs:

God/Spirituality Is a Helpful/Healing Source/Resource for Therapy (39.1 Percent)

- "Need to go beyond simply dependence on will power or returning to thinking/behavior to effect 'second order change,' Jung's belief that real change requires some kind of spiritual change."
- "That He is the ultimate healer."
- "I do not use the word God, but I believe that complete recovery from the severe abuse my clients have suffered ultimately requires a sense of spirituality."
- "For those who believe, God's power and love are effective agents for change."
- "Spirituality is fundamental to health, spirituality is as crucial to health as rational thinking or healthy bodies, or problem-solving skills."

God/Spirituality Is an Important Aspect of Human Life (38.4 Percent)

- "Importance of reliance on a 'power greater than self.'"
- "God is the guiding power behind all happiness and joy in life."
- "Belief in the importance of a spiritual aspect of life."
- "I believe spirituality is an important component of one's life and should be nourished."
- "Spirituality is what integrates life—so therapy is incomplete if it doesn't attend to all dimensions of life."

Personal Theory Supports Client-Initiated Conversation (22.5 Percent)

- "Whatever my client brings in is discussible."
- "I am very open and willing to discuss what is of central importance to my client and to be respectful of their views."
- "N/A except when client introduces."
- "If it is important to the client I don't believe that therapy is complete without it. I believe that a therapist must attempt to enter into the 'world' of the client."
- "If spiritual/religious issues are important to the client to talk about, I would respond to that need/want."

TABLE 10.1. Responses to "What assumptions and/or beliefs do you have that encouraged you to talk about God in therapy?"

Theme	LMFT (*n* = 75)	Psych. (*n* = 76)	Total (*n* = 151)
God/spirituality is a helpful/healing source/resource for therapy	37 (49.3%)	22 (28.9%)	59 (39.1%)
God/spirituality is an important aspect of human life	29 (38.6%)	29 (38.2%)	58 (38.4%)
Personal theory supporting client-initiated conversation	15 (20.0%)	19 (25.0%)	34 (22.5%)

Note: LMFT = licensed marriage and family therapist; Psych. = licensed psychologist

These results indicate that many therapists readily acknowledge that certain beliefs and/or assumptions they hold influence their openness to discussing spiritual and/or religious issues in psychotherapy. These findings are important because they provide some insight into the thought processes of therapists who are willing to integrate religion, spirituality, and psychotherapy. It was important to learn from the therapists who were discouraged from entering into discussions of this kind in therapy. It is also important to learn from the therapists who have been encouraged to enter into spiritual conversations in therapy. Research clearly indicates that therapists have been encouraged to enter into discussions about God in therapy by holding beliefs such as: (1) God and spirituality can be a helpful and/or healing resource for therapy, (2) God and spirituality are important aspects of human life, and (3) clients should be able to initiate topics to be discussed in therapy.

This should not be surprising since we've previously discussed the fact that research demonstrates that the personal beliefs of therapists can influence their behavior in therapy. Rocket science, this is not. However, many therapists who supposedly support client-directed therapy, demonstrate through their practice that they actually only "selectively" support this concept. This is unfortunate considering that therapists can learn a great deal about therapeutic processes from simply paying attention to what clients are teaching them. Many clients not only believe in God, they also believe that God can be a powerfully helpful source of healing and help in the therapeutic process. We hope professionals in the mental health field never get so prideful and/or narcissistic that they become unwilling to learn from their clients. Indeed, our clients can teach us a great deal about therapy!

Chapter 11

Learning from Our Clients

The only person who is educated is the one who has learned how to learn and change.

Carl Rogers

IS INTEGRATION INEVITABLE?

Empirical research demonstrates that numerous therapists have been encouraged by their clients to talk about God in therapy. As discussed in Chapter 10, empirical research involving clients themselves also demonstrates that many clients want to talk about spiritual issues in therapy. For practitioners, this is no surprise. The reality is that, even without therapists initiating such discussions, clients often talk about God and their faith when discussing the life issues with which they are dealing. The evidence is so overwhelming, it should no longer be surprising to the nonpracticing therapists who are academic trainers of therapists. (We successfully resist the temptation to go on a Millerian-like rant on this too-often-seen training reality.) However, a person does not have to be a practicing therapist to understand some of the reasons why God talk in therapy is so common.

1. Ninety-five percent of Americans believe in God (Gallup, 2001).
2. Over 90 percent of Americans affiliate themselves with, and participate in, organized religion (Gallup, 2001).
3. Many therapists report clients bring up God in therapy (Kahle, 1997).
4. Clients report they would prefer a therapeutic experience in which their spiritual orientation is welcomed and respected (Goedde, 2001).

5. Religious clients are more likely to refer their religious friends to a counselor who supported their beliefs rather than to a counselor who challenged their beliefs (McCullough and Worthington, 1995).
6. Most Americans (i.e., "potential clients") would prefer a counselor who *is* religious (Gallup Poll Monthly, 1993)!

Friends, like it or not, if you're a counselor in America, you will be confronted with God talk in therapy. Therefore, it's important to become well informed about how you can participate in these conversations in both ethical and helpful ways. Two of the ways you can do this are: (1) learn what research is telling us about clients/potential clients, and (2) learn what our clients are telling us themselves.

Toward these two goals, let's first address a very important question. We understand that many clients want to include spiritual issues in therapy. However, we've yet to address an issue that is perhaps even more important than the fact that many clients desire this type of integrated therapeutic approach. Some may ask, "How can any issue be more important than the fact that clients want these conversations to occur in therapy?" We would respond that research demonstrates that the beliefs of therapists on this very issue in question influence their willingness to address spiritual issues in therapy, regardless of whether or not their clients want to discuss spiritual issues in therapy.

Can spirituality, religion, and/or God be a helpful and/or healing source in effectively helping clients attain their therapeutic goals?

IS INTEGRATION HELPFUL?

Propst and colleagues (1992) demonstrated that depressed religious clients who participated in either religiously adapted cognitive-behavioral therapy (CBT) or pastoral counseling reported significantly lower posttreatment depression scores and greater improvement in social adjustment than did religious clients who participated in standard CBT. Of note was the finding that the treatment participants that reported the best gains were those who participated in religiously adapted CBT with nonreligious therapists (Propst et al., 1992). These results supported a previous study that found CBT religious imagery treatment and group discussion of religious issues as more effective in decreasing symptoms of depression than CBT nonreligious imagery treatment (Propst, 1980). Based on these results, Propst and colleagues (1992) suggest, "That a religious treatment delivery system itself may have a therapeutic impact regardless of whether any supposed active ingredients of CBT are present" (p. 101). This theory is consistent with findings that demonstrated that religious clients often responded more positively to cognitive restructuring of distorted thinking when it was based on scripture rather than only on empirical evidence or reason (Tan, 1987).

More recent research demonstrates the powerful impact that integrating spirituality can have on the therapeutic process (Cole, 2000; Nohr, 2001). A fascinating study by Brenda Cole (2000) found that cancer patients who took part in a spiritually focused therapy (SFT) group fared much better than patients who were in a no-treatment control group (NTC). Results demonstrated that over the course of treatment, severity of pain increased for the NTC group, and severity of pain decreased for the SFT group. Results also demonstrated that the SFT group's level of depression remained fairly stable over time while the NTC group's level of depression increased. Finally, the findings of this study also supported the importance of spiritual coping activities. For example, surrendering control (to God) was predictive of lower levels of pain severity, anxiety, and depression; higher quality of life; and fewer physical symptoms.

These findings challenge the old notion put forth by some people within our field, who dichotomized locus of control and made related assumptive assertions, that religion supports ideas that are counter to healthy approaches to life. We call this the "internal locus of control = good; external locus of control = bad" assumption. Based on these findings, other empirical findings, and our own clinical experience, we believe that many people benefit from a therapeutic approach that appropriately respects the concepts of an internal locus of control, an external locus of control, and an interrelated transcendent locus of control.

We will address this in greater depth shortly, but digress with us for a moment. Ever wonder if the theorist who first differentiated between internal and external loci of control had control issues? Robert Nohr (2001) found that participants in both a spiritually integrated cognitive-behavioral-technique workshop (SCBT) and in a standard CBT stress-management workshop demonstrated significant improvement on a symptom checklist after attending these workshops. Interestingly, participants in the SCBT condition exhibited a trend toward greater maintenance of well-being status when compared to the participants in the CBT condition. Empirical research findings suggest that integrating spirituality and treatment can have a positive therapeutic impact on clients who are seeking treatment for depression, cancer, anxiety, pain management, and stress. This would seem important for all therapists to understand, perhaps especially those participants in our study who indicated they may have avoided talking about God in therapy because they believed that a discussion in therapy about spirituality is not helpful, harmful, and/or inappropriate. Indeed, research *about* clients can be very effective in informing us about potential pathways that can be helpful in therapy. Interestingly, some within our field are discovering that research *including* our clients may provide even more information about how helpful integrating spirituality and therapy can be.

DO CLIENTS BELIEVE IT'S HELPFUL TO INCLUDE SPIRITUALITY IN THERAPY?

Several of our colleagues have commented that they believe it's unethical for therapists to expect their clients to educate them. We understand the spirit in which they make such statements. However, without a clarifying differentiation on this point, some people might believe them. This would be a grave error. In fact, we would argue that an interchange between a therapist and a client in which the therapist was not learning from his or her client could not be classified as therapy. Perhaps it would be some form of narcissistic dialogue, but not therapy.

Yet we agree that it is inappropriate in certain situations to expect our clients to educate us. It is a therapist's responsibility to strive toward competence through further education, supervision, and/or consultation. Indeed, a therapist who did not take steps toward becoming more competent on a certain subject, but depended solely on clients to educate him or her, would be acting in a less-than-competent manner. For example, a less-than-competent therapist might think, "I didn't really know much about Bob's issues because he is African American. Hey, my client Mary is also African American. I'll spend some time in our next session asking her several questions about what it's like to be an African American so I can learn how to better work with

Bob." This is not exactly what the ethical guidelines were stating related to "have or obtain the training, experience, consultation, or supervision necessary to ensure the competence of their services" (APA, 2002, p. 1064).

Although we believe it could be unethical to expect our clients to educate us, we believe that it is incumbent upon us, as therapists, to learn from our clients. This may sound quite elementary based on the fact that our work so often centers on asking clients questions to obtain information about their unique lives. However, you might be surprised how many therapists have mistakenly blended, "It is inappropriate to expect our clients to educate us," into "It is inappropriate to expect us to learn from our clients." In fact, we have learned a great deal about the therapeutic process from our clients. In so doing, we have learned about the integration of spirituality and psychotherapy.

A former client described the interrelated transcendent locus of control very well in a letter of thanks he wrote to me (PK) months after his treatment had ended. He wanted me to know that he was still doing very well. In this letter, he wrote,

> I have always had faith in God. My whole life I believed in Jesus. I believed that he was with me. With the help of you and faith-based therapy, now I KNOW that I am not alone. I KNOW that God is with me. There is a huge difference between believing and knowing. . . . There is no way I could have broken free from the bondage of depression on my own or just with the help of a therapist. But you helped me to see that "I can do all things through Christ who strengthens me" (Philippians 4:13). You see, in order to turn my life around I did not need to make a 180-degree turn. I only needed to make a 90-degree turn and focus upward on Jesus. The peace that man gives is temporary, but the true peace that Jesus gives lasts for eternity.

The content of this letter may be quite intense and/or uncomfortable for some therapists to read. However, make no mistake this client believed it was helpful to include his spiritual faith in his therapeutic work that focused on decreasing the influence of depression in his life. Many other clients have also found it helpful to integrate their spirituality and psychotherapy.

Adam Coffey (2001) found that clients viewed spirituality as central to their therapy experiences either a priori or retrospectively.

Coffey utilized ethnographic interviews with a number of psychotherapy clients to explore their actual views regarding the integration of spirituality and their therapeutic work. More and more researchers are using ethnography and other qualitative methods to gather important information directly from clients rather than relying on their own assumptive theories about what helped clients during the course of therapy. Based on his findings, Coffey concludes that "implicit and explicit experiences of spirituality in couples therapy improved both the therapeutic process and outcome" (p. 178). This researcher also asserted that the literature on the integration of spirituality and therapy has historically relied too heavily on theoretical distinctions and has only recently started to incorporate the perspectives of clients. We completely agree with Coffey's assertions.

On more than one occasion, we have witnessed therapeutic encounters in which the therapist's theoretical orientation seemed to get in the way of therapy. These theory-saturated encounters have led us to be leery of theory blindedness. As therapists, we need to guard against analysis paralysis, intellectual narcissism, and self-centeredness in therapy. For if we don't, we may run the risk of imposing our theoretical and epistemological orientations on to the client. This could easily create a blind spot where we wouldn't even think to ask ourselves very simple, yet important questions such as,

- What is the client seeking in therapy?
- What is the client's epistemological source?
- What is it that my client is telling me?

Several years ago, we were both involved in a training exercise in which we used a pseudoethnographic interview with some of our clients to learn more about their perception of the therapeutic process. These interviews proved to be very informative and helpful because we learned some things that really challenged some of our assumptions and beliefs about what works in therapy and what is in the best interests of our clients. In one such interview with a mother and her son, Chantel and William, we were surprised to find out what they found to be most helpful in their therapeutic work with Peter. In fact, we learned quite a bit from William and Chantel. They were gracious enough to give us permission to share their story with you.

CHANTEL AND WILLIAM

Chantel, a thirty-two-year-old single mother, first presented to therapy with her twelve-year-old biological son, William. Chantel reported that William's father had very minimal contact with William and was not providing them with any financial assistance. Chantel was employed full-time and was also taking a significant number of college credit hours. She reported that William had recently been expelled from his school and was sent to an alternative educational facility because his school principal had reported that he had sexually harassed one of his female classmates. Chantel said that William had supposedly dropped something on the ground so he could look up a girl's dress. Chantel reported that she was concerned about her son's impulse control because he had also gotten into trouble at school for talking excessively in class.

We will share more details of their story in Chapter 15, but let's briefly summarize some of the other themes we addressed in therapy with this family unit. Other major issues addressed during the course of therapy were academic performance on exams, learning how to handle the tactics of bullies, improving communication inside the home, and grieving the death of a close family member.

The following transcript was taken directly from the video of the pseudoethnographic interview with Chantel and William at the conclusion of Peter's work with this family. We were blessed to have the talented Bonnie Osmon, past president of the Arkansas Association for Marriage and Family Therapy, as the interviewer during this interview session. This is not a transcript from the entire interview. Chantel and William had both already reported earlier in the interview that they thought the therapeutic process was very helpful. Bonnie did not initiate the discussion of spirituality in therapy. The topic came up as Chantel was answering a question that Bonnie had posed to her, "What did you and William bring into therapy that helped the therapeutic process be successful?"

Excerpt from Transcript of Interview

BONNIE: You were saying that one of the things you brought to therapy was that you were honest with Peter. I guess I was going off on a track because I think I know what you mean. Were you frank with Peter?

CHANTEL: I didn't have to hide anything.

BONNIE: You didn't have to?

CHANTEL: No. I mean you didn't feel like you had to hide anything. He made it comfortable. You just didn't feel like you had to hide anything . . . and especially I remember one time we came to him and spoke about God and you didn't have to hide things and you weren't judged on your religion or your faith. It was like you can be open about it.

BONNIE: You said that with your faith you were open about it. What is your advice to therapists about how they can talk with their clients about that part of their life, too?

CHANTEL: I just think you have to be open because people come from . . . they have different religions, they have different faiths. I guess you have to be open to it and not be judgmental about what faith they come from. If you don't quite understand it maybe you can expand upon it to where you can go and say, "Maybe I can help you later on" if you don't quite understand about their faith or their religion or whatever they bring to you.

BONNIE: Even if you don't know someone else's religion or faith, to find out something about it and say, "I can't say much about it right now"?

CHANTEL: Yeah! But by all means let them express themselves and if you still don't quite understand it, that is OK also, but then maybe next time after you have investigated it, then you can be more aware of it.

BONNIE: Were there some ways that you can remember that Peter talked to you that day (in a session talking about the death of a family member) that helped you talk about that?

CHANTEL: I don't know, it just seemed like we started . . . I don't know how. We just thought about getting it out . . . I guess it was just comfortable. You just felt like you could.

BONNIE: OK. What was there about Peter, that he did or said, that made it comfortable to talk about your faith?

CHANTEL: I can remember one incident when I thought William was going to hold back one time, when William took the TAAS exam, and he had . . . I didn't think he had done his best so I was really upset with him and Peter asked him that if he [William] was there writing it [his TAAS essay] now, what would we [Chantel and Peter] see? William started giving this example of Lazo and Akelia and he [William] said, "But if I say it you might think I'm crazy!" And he [Peter] is like, "Well no. You are not crazy." Well, then, he [William] goes on to tell us about this, this Lazo that tapped him on the shoulder . . . he [William] looked one way, then he looked the other. And then he went on to talk about Akelia and that is what I am saying because Peter went on and said, "Well, who is Akelia?" . . . and then William went on to explain to him, "Well, Akelia is this." And he [Peter] encouraged him in a way that it is OK to tell me. Then William went on to say, "I guess God is the supreme Akelia" and it was cultured and coercive where it was OK to say and no it wasn't crazy to say.

BONNIE: So he listened in a way that made it seem as though you didn't feel Peter was thinking, "Oh, this guy is from left field"?

CHANTEL: Yeah.

BONNIE: But it was more as though he was taking it seriously. Listening, asking more questions, like explain this to me more?

CHANTEL: Yeah!

We learned a great deal from these clients. Chantel very clearly stated that she and her son had a very positive experience with therapy that integrated their spiritual faith into their therapeutic work. She commented that, rather than feeling as though they were judged or made to feel crazy, they felt comfortable talking about their faith in therapy. Exploring this further, take particular note of the interchange related to how the subject of spirituality was initiated in therapy and how Peter may have participated in this process. Chantel reported, "I don't know, it just seemed like we started . . . I don't know how. We just thought about getting it out . . . I guess it was just comfortable. You just felt like you could."

This information can be very helpful to therapists and therapists in training since some therapists believe you need to have techniques or interventions designed to make clients talk about spirituality. We don't believe these are the most helpful ways therapists can work with clients around issues of spirituality in therapy. Instead, we take positions of respect, acceptance, and curiosity with regard to our clients in which we offer them what we, based on Jenkins' work, call invitations to authenticity.

This frees us up from the limitations of the frequently assumed artificial dichotomy that either "The Therapist Must Initiate Discussions of Spirituality in Therapy" or "The Client Must Initiate Discussions of Spirituality in Therapy." Some may wonder, "Are these authors suggesting that someone other than the therapist or client can initiate a conversation in therapy?" No, this is not what we're suggesting. We simply are suggesting that sometimes it's not easy to determine whether the client or the therapist actually initiated a conversation about spirituality. For example, whom do you believe initiated a conversation about spirituality in the following example?

EXPLICITLY IMPLICIT INTEGRATION, IMPLICITLY EXPLICIT INTEGRATION, OR . . . ?

CLIENT: Recently, I haven't felt as good on some days as I have on others.

THERAPIST: Would you please tell me more about the days when you felt better?

CLIENT: Well, it just seems that some days I feel better about myself than I do on other days. I'm not exactly sure why this is the case.

THERAPIST: What types of things have you done to invite peace into your life on those days when you've felt better?

CLIENT: It may be that I'm more intentional about my prayer life on the days when I feel better about myself. Maybe that's part of it.

THERAPIST: What is it about your prayer life that you find helpful?

CLIENT: Well, I think that prayer helps me experience greater peace in my life because my focus is more on God than it is on all the little things that I really don't have any control over anyway. This helps me focus on what God has done for me rather than worrying about what I need to do for God. You know . . .

We agree with Tan and see the process of integration as falling along an integration continuum. Sometimes spiritual conversations arise in therapy and a person can't be certain who initiated the conversation. Other times, clients initiate conversations about spiritual issues in therapy. Still other times, we might say something such as, "In light of the research on anxiety and depression that suggests that mental, physical, and spiritual balance in a person's life can help improve his or her quality of life, we may want to explore the implications of this research in your life. Different people do different things within these realms to try to take care of themselves. What types of things do you do to strive toward balance in your own life?"

We very carefully choose the words we use in our questions. In some instances, we may simply include a word such as "peace, love, or belief" in a general question to see if it may help us to learn information about the client that may aid the therapeutic process. Although this can be very useful at times, we do not have to do this very often because it's usually very easy to determine whether spirituality is an important part of a client's life by simply paying attention to what the client says during therapy.

ATTENDING TO CLIENTS' WORDS

> *Without knowing the force of words, it is impossible to know men.*
>
> Confucius

Words are a very powerful source in therapy. With this in mind, we believe that words can either help or hurt the work of a therapist. Needless to say, it's very important to pay attention to the words that our clients use, whether or not we are discussing spiritual issues in therapy. For example, if a client uses the word *God* to describe his or her spiritual source, the client may be turned off if the therapist follows such a statement with a question such as, "Will you tell me more about your higher power?" That being said, if a client uses the term *higher power,* the therapist would be wise to avoid asking a follow-up question about God. By paying close attention to the words clients use in therapy, attentive therapists can learn a great deal about their clients' beliefs and how they may prefer to be worked with in therapy.

This linguistic attentiveness can also help therapists hear, and influence them to act on, potential invitations to authenticity from their clients. These clues, so to speak, can help therapists answer important questions such as, "What seems important to this client? Should I talk about spirituality with this client? Does it appear that this client wants to talk about spirituality in therapy? How should I talk about spirituality with this client?"

Our belief that words are a potentially powerful source of influence on the therapeutic process influenced us to ask the participants in our study a couple of open-ended questions to further explore this belief. We were able to get some very important information from responses to the question, "What words, when you hear them, would encourage you in therapy to talk about the client's described God?" (see Table 11.1).

Participants used some of the following comments to describe key words:

Reference to God, a Deity, or a Higher Power (50.3 Percent)

- "God, Higher Power . . ."
- "God, Jesus Christ . . ."
- "Higher power, God within, someone up there, God (and all references to God), Heavenly Father, Yaweh, etc."
- "God, Holy Spirit, Jesus, Blessed, Allah, Jehovah, Yaweh."

TABLE 11.1. Responses to "What words, when you hear them, would encourage you in therapy to talk about the client's described God?"

Theme	LMFT (n = 75)	Psych. (n = 76)	Total (n = 151)
Reference to God, a deity, or a higher power	43 (57.3%)	33 (43.4%)	76 (50.3%)
Religious terms, religious participation/affiliation	26 (34.7%)	26 (34.2%)	52 (34.4%)
Expressions of faith/belief	29 (38.6%)	21 (27.6%)	50 (33.1%)
Specific presenting issue/problem	17 (22.7%)	17 (22.4%)	34 (22.5%)
Reference to spirituality	16 (21.3%)	14 (18.4%)	30 (19.9%)
Search for meaning/clarity/ significance in life	11 (14.6%)	17 (22.4%)	28 (18.5%)
Any words when initiated by client	13 (17.3%)	9 (11.8%)	22 (14.6%)

Note: LMFT = licensed marriage and family therapist; Psych. = licensed psychologist

Religious Terms, Religious Participation/Affiliation (34.4 Percent)

- "Any mentioned religion, church, the Bible, pro or con."
- "Regular church attendance, Bible study, Bible reading."
- "Church, Sunday school, mass, religion, bible study."
- "Indirectly stated values (discussion of worship participation, group membership)."
- "My religious/spiritual belief, I'm religious, I'm a Christian."

Expressions of Faith/Belief (33.1 Percent)

- "Any expression of belief, faith . . ."
- "Pray, prayer, belief."
- "God can help me, I know he can."
- "My faith in God is very strong."
- "Prayer is important to me! Without my faith I could not have made [it] through this time."

Specific Presenting Issue/Problem (22.5 Percent)

- "Any words that I felt might aid the client in a grieving situation."
- "Hopelessness, need to be loved, guilt, hate."
- "Death, kill myself."
- "[When] a pt. is discouraged, hopeless, alone, terminal—often bring up their ideas of God."
- "Death, suicide, aging."
- "Guilt, involvement in AA or Alanon."

Reference to Spirituality (19.9 Percent)

- "Any mention on part of client about . . . spirituality."
- "Any questions or references to . . . spirituality."
- "Client: 'I am confused and feel guilty about my belief in God or my spirituality.'"
- "When they introduce spiritual theme, talk about their beliefs & how they influence their choices, decisions, etc."
- "Any reference to client's loss of relationship with their spiritual life."

Search for Meaning, Clarity, Significance in Life (18.5 Percent)

- "That they feel a spiritual void or feel confused or conflicted."
- "It's hopeless, life has no meaning."
- "Existential crisis."
- "Meaning, purpose, destiny . . ."
- "Emptiness, no meaning in life, lost sense of purpose, no direction."

Any Words When Initiated by Client (14.6 Percent)

- "If the client brought it up I would try to facilitate them talking—just as I would re: any other topic."
- "Anything they say on the topic."
- "In general, if a client brings up the subject I discuss it."
- "Nothing in particular, if they had not raised the issue themselves in some way."
- "Anything s/he says that are related. I take an accepting, reflective approach."

Clearly, these results suggest that certain spoken words and verbalized beliefs can encourage therapists to enter into spiritual discussions with their clients in therapy. These results suggest that the behavior of therapists can be influenced by both the words that clients speak in therapy and the meaning therapists make of these spoken words. Therefore, it's important for therapists to be aware of the influence that certain spoken words can have on them as therapists, as well as on the therapeutic process in general. If therapists are aware of this, they can, indeed, learn a great deal about their clients and about potential therapeutic pathways from simply attending to the words spoken by their clients.

Given this information, therapists can also learn from certain clients' spoken words which topics may *not* be potential therapeutic pathways for their work with them. You likely have our routine down by now. Yes, we simply changed one word again. And again, we found some interesting information from the responses to the question, "What words, when you hear them, would discourage you in therapy to talk about the client's described God?" (see Table 11.2).

TABLE 11.2. Responses to "What words, when you hear them, would discourage you in therapy to talk about the client's described God?"

Theme	LMFT (*n* = 75)	Psych. (*n* = 76)	Total (*n* = 151)
Client is not religious/does not believe in God	21 (28.0%)	16 (21.1%)	37 (24.5%)
Client has negative view of God/religion	15 (20.0%)	14 (18.4%)	29 (19.2%)
Client states a desire not to talk about God, religion, and/or spirituality	15 (20.0%)	7 (9.2%)	22 (14.6%)
None	9 (12.0%)	12 (15.8%)	21 (13.9%)
Client's states beliefs are perceived as rigid/dysfunctional	6 (8.0%)	10 (13.2%)	16 (10.6%)

Note: LMFT = licensed marriage and family therapist; Psych. = licensed psychologist

Participants used some of the following comments to describe key words:

Client Is Not Religious/Does Not Believe in God (24.5 Percent)

- "Person saying they are not religious."
- "I'm an atheist/agnostic, God does not exist."
- "I don't believe in God."
- "Any expression of disbelief. I will not 'fight' with the client about spiritual issues."

Client Has Negative View of God/Religion (19.2 Percent)

- "Evidence of disaffection with, mistreatment at the hands of, indifference to religious experience or institution—evidence of negative or skeptical belief system of God."
- "I had that stuff crammed down my throat when I was a kid."
- "Anger resentment toward religion."
- "Slams on church people."
- "That damn church, screw religion, those do-gooders, those busy bodies at church."

Client States a Desire Not to Talk About God, Religion, and/or Spirituality (14.6 Percent)

- "If the client says that they do not wish to discuss this topic in therapy."
- "Don't talk to me about God, the Bible, church."
- "My spiritual life is personal and private. I do not choose to discuss spiritual issues."
- " 'I don't want to talk about God or spiritual things.'—Respect boundaries set by client."
- "I don't believe in god and I don't want to hear god-talk."

None (13.9 Percent)

- "I can't think of a time when this would come up."
- "Nothing discourages me."
- "None if that is where the client wants to go."
- "None. If I heard them we could explore them because the client first brought up the words related to God."

Client's Stated Beliefs Are Seen As Rigid/Dysfunctional (10.6 Percent)

- "Any rigid use of scripture that paints people and situations as black & white."
- "Doctrinaire opinionated beliefs which are dysfunctional."
- "A dogmatic religious belief (i.e., 'the Bible says it so it must be true.' That leaves little room for exploration with a client) that appears to have little to do with therapeutic goals."
- "God just wants us to be happy—no one can tell me what to do—God understands and forgives me no matter what I do."
- "Strident desire to proselytize."
- "When a client appears to be fanatical in a belief system and uses words that describe absolution such as—My religion is the only true one. God is a punishing overseer of human behavior."

Once again, the responses to this question provide some very interesting information. It appears that therapists can be deterred from having spiritual discussions in therapy by certain spoken words and/or beliefs espoused by clients during therapy. This isn't surprising.

However, we found the responses to this particular question especially informative.

It's clear that some therapists would not be discouraged from entering into spiritual conversations by any words they might hear in therapy. This could be potentially dangerous, if their clients do not want to talk about God in therapy or have had very negative religious/spiritual experiences in the past. If a therapist must talk about God in therapy with every client, no matter whether or not the client wants to talk about God, we would simply ask that type of therapist to examine his or her motivation in mandating God talk in therapy.

Second, some therapists indicated that they would be discouraged from entering into spiritual conversations with their clients in therapy based on how they viewed their clients' espoused beliefs. This could also be a potentially dangerous situation, if the therapist defines rigid and/or dysfunctional, whether intentionally or not, as beliefs that are different than his or her own spiritual beliefs. We would ask that type of therapist to examine the basis on which he or she determined whether spiritual beliefs were dysfunctional or rigid. Indeed, such an examination might reveal to some therapists the existence of their own rigid, and perhaps dysfunctional, criteria by which they had defined rigid and dysfunctional.

The responses to these questions suggest that it's extremely important for all therapists to learn from their clients. However, the responses to these questions continue to suggest that the ability of therapists to be helpful to their clients may be directly related to how well they're able to self-reflexively learn about themselves. For, indeed, therapists have the power to hurt the therapeutic process when working with spiritual and/or religious clients. Yet therapists also have the power to help create an environment that can be amazingly therapeutic for their spiritual clients.

Chapter 12

The Power to Help

God is our refuge and strength, an ever-present help in trouble.

King David,
Psalm 46:1

Although we don't believe there's a "how-to manual" with regard to integrating spirituality and psychotherapy, we do believe that there are certain things that therapists can do to invite healthy and helpful conversations about spirituality into the therapeutic process. By no means do we guarantee that if a therapist does these things, helpful and healthy conversations will automatically take place. Since we're mammals, we, too, are limited by the truth of the Serenity Prayer . . . we can't control that which we can't control. However, it's by acknowledging the reality of this limitation that we experience the freedom with which to work with our clients. Therefore, we offer the following ten principles, in no particular order of significance, as things that therapists can do to be therapeutically helpful when working with clients who want to address spiritual and/or religious issues in therapy.

TEN WAYS THERAPISTS CAN SUPPORT SPIRITUAL HEALTH IN THERAPY

1. Examine your own beliefs regarding spirituality and religion.

Examine your own spiritual and/or religious beliefs. It can be a very helpful process of discovering things about yourself and your beliefs that may benefit you, your family, your friends, and your clients. Although we both (PK and JR) grew up in Christian homes, it wasn't really until we were adults that we challenged ourselves to explore why we held the beliefs we held. On one Sunday around the time I was completing my graduate work, I (PK) visited a church in which I was not a member. During that service, a verse was read that helped challenge me to explore my beliefs. "Always be prepared to give an answer to everyone who asks you to give the reason for the hope that you have. But do this with gentleness and respect" (I Peter 3:15, NIV). Until then, if someone would have asked me why I believed what I believed, I would have probably become frustrated. Although I believed in God, if I were to have honestly given an answer to the person posing such a question, I would have had to articulate something profound, such as "Because the Bible says so" or "Because that's what I believe." Not exactly the words that would have given someone a clear impression of why I personally believed as I did. After hearing this scripture, I realized that I had a responsibility to myself and to others to examine my beliefs. This process led me to read extensively, many different books by many different authors, and to have extensive conversations with people whom I respect. As a result of this examination, I now understand why I have the hope that I do and I can articulate the reasons for this hope with gentleness and respect, rather than fumbling and stumbling with frustration. The good news is that the examination continues.

2. Become aware of the impact that your own beliefs can have on a therapeutic conversation.

Accept the reality that *your own beliefs about spirituality and religion can and will impact how you address spiritual issues in therapy.* We overtly acknowledge that our belief that God can be a helpful and healing source in life makes us more willing than some others to talk about spirituality in therapy. It's important to learn about, and own, your beliefs, because research has demonstrated that the behavior of therapists with regard to the explicit integration of religion and psychotherapy is influenced by their personal views of religion (Shafranske and Malony, 1990; Kahle, 1997).

An interesting note from our study was the finding that a significantly larger proportion of extrinsically religious respondents than intrinsically religious respondents and indiscriminately proreligious respondents, indicated that they were not willing to introduce the topic of spirituality in psychotherapy. Also, the intrinsically religious, indiscriminately proreligious, and indiscriminately nonreligious respondent groups were all significantly more willing to introduce the topic of spirituality in psychotherapy than were their extrinsically religious colleagues. Perhaps practitioners who are intrinsically religious, indiscriminately proreligious, and indiscriminately nonreligious may be clearer about their beliefs with regard to God, spirituality, and/or religion and, therefore, are less threatened when people talk about beliefs that are different than their own. Since extrinsically religious individuals simply "use" religion as a means for socializing (Allport and Ross, 1967), perhaps they are not as likely to consider God and/or spirituality a potential source of comfort or healing.

Tan (1996) asserted that therapists who practice from an explicit model are usually religious themselves. In light of the findings of our study, perhaps it may be more appropriate to say that individuals who practice from an explicit model may be individuals who are clear about their religious and/or spiritual beliefs, regardless of whether or not they are religious themselves. An additional finding from our study demonstrated that religious orientation was also significantly related to the degree to which respondents were willing to talk about spirituality, even when the client introduced the topic. In summary, the beliefs of the therapist are a potential and real source of influence.

3. Respect your clients' passion for their spiritual and/or religious faith.

We believe that it is not enough to simply respect your clients' beliefs. We think it is also important to respect their passion and/or the importance they place on their beliefs. Many individuals believe that their relationship with God is the most important thing in their lives. We have heard many people over the years say things such as, "God first, family second, work third" in response to a question related to the most important thing in their lives. Fully understanding a client's beliefs necessitates gaining an understanding of the importance of the client's beliefs in his or her life. Hence, we believe that it is only possible for a therapist to respect the beliefs of his or her client if he or she also respects the client's passion for his or her beliefs. Unfortunately, many therapists are only able to respect people's beliefs up to a certain point.

I (JR) was involved in a group-interview process one time during which a therapist's faith in God was raised as an issue by one of the individuals. One of the interviewees had formerly been a minister in a Christian denomination. During the postinterview discussion about the interviewee, one of the therapists who was involved in the selection process said, "I'm OK that he is a Christian, but I think that he may be too strong of a Christian." A discussion ensued in which the strength of this man's faith was actually viewed by some others as a deficit, too. Apparently this man would have been a better candidate in the eyes of some had he been a "half-ass Christian" instead of a Christian who cared deeply about his faith. Apparently, some therapists value the motto, "Faith, but only in moderation." We believe this says a great deal more about these professionals' comfort zones, which are related to their own beliefs, than it does about this man's faith. This fairly common belief in the mental health fields, although very subtle, is a value imposition waiting to happen. In fact, in that interview process it did happen.

4. Respect the fact that your clients can have their own spiritual beliefs, even if you don't agree with them nor support their espoused beliefs. Understand that respect, support, and agreement are not synonymous.

Spiritual agreement is not a necessary requirement for a therapeutic relationship. If total agreement on every life issue were a necessary requirement for a therapeutic relationship, therapy would cease to exist. There are many different religions and many different perspectives on these religions. Even within the realms of Christianity, there are reasons for numerous denominations. Understand the fact that you will not necessarily agree with every spiritual belief your client may hold.

We've seen some colleagues erroneously equate respect and support with agreement. This is a very dangerous proposition and a trap waiting for us to take its bait. During simple disagreements on an issue, we've heard people say things such as, "That's what I believe, and I can't believe you are not respecting me and supporting me." Often times, what they're really saying is, "The only way I'll think that you're respecting and supporting me is if you change your mind to believe what I believe." The astute therapist would be wise to avoid setting this trap as well as avoid being caught in it. Spiritual agreement is not a necessary requirement for a therapeutic relationship in which spiritual issues are discussed.

5. Honor the potentially positive and negative power of religion in people's lives.

I (JR) consulted on an interesting case back in 1999. A currently separated, young married woman, Caroline, sought help in trying to deal with some issues she was confronted with in her marriage. Caroline reported that her husband, L. D., had become involved in a cult approximately a year after they were married. She reported that when she returned home from a two-week medical mission trip out of the country, L. D. invited her to attend a gathering at the home of a leader of a new church he wanted them to attend. Caroline reported that she agreed to attend, and so they went to this church gathering. Upon entering the church leader's home, Caroline was instructed to go to another room with the other women so the men could discuss important matters. Not knowing anyone else at this gathering other than L. D., Caroline decided to stay with her husband, which apparently was not received well by the men. Caroline reported that the leader and the other men would not acknowledge her despite the fact that she tried to engage herself in the conversation on numerous occasions. Later, when they left the gathering, Caroline told L. D., "Something is not right there. I felt very weird the entire time we were there." She also told L. D. that she was uncomfortable with some of the teachings espoused by the leader, to which her husband suggested that she was simply overreacting.

Over the next several weeks, L. D. became more involved in this church and she became more and more alarmed. L. D. soon told Caroline that she would not be allowed to work outside of the home any longer because he believed that it was against God's teachings. Why? Because L. D. believed that women must be protected from temptation.

I was given a letter written by L. D. to read. In this letter, he said that as the husband, he had complete authority over his wife "in much the same way as the slave and master." He wrote, "She is not left to make even the decision of a vow on her own unless she is widowed." In this letter, L. D. quoted many verses from the Bible in an attempt to assert that the Bible supported all of his beliefs. Beliefs such as, "Women are more susceptible to temptation and sin than are men," and, since Caroline disagreed with his interpretation of scripture, "We must understand that she is in direct rebellion to God."

Caroline reported that L. D. had verbally and emotionally abused her since joining this church, even suggesting that she was walking with Satan, not God, because she disagreed with him. He wrote in this letter,

> Would it be loving for me to just allow this to go on or would it be a display of my love to make sure that it doesn't. Furthermore, as the head of my house I must deal with this to prevent my house from self-destructing (doesn't Jesus teach that a house divided against itself will surely fall). . . . If I, as the head of my house, allow this to go on, I, too, will be held responsible.

Although Caroline did not mention this form of abuse, we also believed she was experiencing a form of spiritual abuse and, based on the letter and other information, we were concerned that there was a potential danger of physical abuse.

We both hypothesized that Caroline's faith in God had likely taken a hit as a result of what she was experiencing. However, I (JR) soon found out that we were very wrong. In response to the question, "What's helping you deal with what you are going through?" Caroline responded, "My faith in God." She went on to say that just as some individuals have to deal with physical cancer, some individuals are confronted with other challenges in life. "I don't know why I'm going through what I'm going through, but my faith in Jesus Christ as my savior has helped me hold on to His promises that I can do all things through Him and all things will work together for good." Caroline's faith in God was a positive power in her life even during a time when she was powerfully confronted with the negative impact of L. D.'s religious beliefs.

6. Be willing to consider offering your own personal, spiritual views if your clients are open to this.

I (Peter) once worked with a woman who presented to therapy reporting a desire to work on her "second layer of healing." Lisa reported that she was a sexual abuse survivor who had successfully worked in past therapy on her first layer of healing, anger. Lisa started off by saying, "I need to let you know up front that I'm hesitant to be here because of your gender. However, for some reason, I know I'm supposed to be here." I thanked her for sharing her initial concern and affirmed the strength she had demonstrated by informing me of this concern. Lisa reported that she saw the second layer of her recovery as "learning to value myself."

A number of sessions into our work together, I asked Lisa, "Has there ever been a time in your life when you have felt valued?" Lisa paused, then she looked down to the ground and continued to pause. After several seconds had passed, she said, still looking down, "I can remember an instance, but I'm hesitant to tell you the story because I don't think we're supposed to talk about spiritual issues in therapy." I responded, "Feel free to share with me whatever it is that you would like to share, regardless of the topic." Lisa then went on to tell me a story of an instance in which she was taking part in a Catholic vigil. (This was somewhat surprising to me because she had previously mentioned some Zen beliefs she had—another reason for therapists to remain curious.) Lisa said that one night she was alone in her church taking her turn in a vigil where members would sit with the host. As she explained, the host is the body of Christ in the form of the postconsecrated unleavened bread used in the sacrament of Holy Communion. Lisa went on to say,

> I was sitting in the front aisle and I had my head bowed, praying to God, asking Him for help as I struggled with ongoing issues related to the sexual abuse I had experienced during my childhood. Then, as I finished my prayer, I looked up and, on the stairs leading up to the altar, I saw a vision of Jesus sitting down surrounded by some sheep. It reminded me of the picture on the cover of a book I had when I was a little girl. Then, I saw Jesus get up and walk toward me.

Lisa had tears coming from her eyes when she paused. She continued, "I looked down, because I was scared. Then I felt the warm touch of His hand on my shoulder. I looked up and Jesus was gone."

Lisa sniffled and took a long pause. Then I asked, "What did this mean to you?" Lisa responded, "It meant that I am a child of God and He loves me." After a long silence, Lisa then said, "I'm sorry. I know people aren't supposed to talk about God in therapy. You probably think that I'm crazy, don't you?" I responded, "No, I don't think you're crazy at all. In fact, I want to tell you that I think you are a very strong person for being able to tell me that story." Lisa smiled as she continued to look down, wiping away some tears with a tissue. I went on to say in a soft voice, "Related to what you mentioned about 'not being able to talk about God in therapy,' I believe that it is important for some people to talk about God in therapy to help them receive the healing help they need." Lisa looked up at me and asked in a surprised yet comforted, tone, "Really?" I said, "Yes. As a matter of fact, I did my dissertation on the integration of spirituality and psychotherapy." Lisa's eyes opened up very wide. She looked shocked. I said, "Are you OK?" Lisa said, "Yes, I am." Then, she smiled and said, "Now I know why I was supposed to see you in therapy. I'm doing my master's thesis on the integration of spirituality and nursing." The hair on the back of my neck stood up at this point.

After a few more sessions, Lisa reported a desire to take a break from therapy. I asked her why she thought this was a good time for a break. She responded with a smile, "Because the second layer of recovery is complete."

> But often clients feel that their private and meaningful conversations with a personal God are unwelcome in the therapy conversation. If we consider this unspoken censoring as a form of professional oppression, though usually inadvertent, then we may see not only how we participate in oppressing but how we can participate in freeing our conversations. (Griffith, 1995b, p. 123)

7. Understand that some clients may prefer a therapist who holds spiritual and/or religious beliefs that are similar to their own beliefs.

As previously mentioned, research indicates that the majority of Americans would prefer a counselor who is religious (Gallup Poll Monthly, 1993). We believe this is partially due to the fact that many Americans believe there is an antireligious bias within the mental health field. We agree with them. Whether you do is, of course, up to you. However, make no mistake: Many potential clients believe there is an antireligious bias in the mental health fields. Perhaps this is a byproduct of Freud's legacy; perhaps it isn't. Regardless, Freud's views on religion did not go unnoticed by the influential Christian thinkers of his time, such as C. S. Lewis.

> Keep clear of psychiatrists unless you know that they are also Christians. Otherwise they start with the assumption that your religion is an illusion and try to "cure" it: and this assumption they make not as professional psychologists but as amateur philosophers. (Lewis, 1947, p. 211)

When I (Peter) was searching for a therapist to conduct my own premarital counseling, finding someone who would be respectful of my spiritual beliefs and the beliefs of my wife to be topped our list of requirements. We didn't ask the counselor we chose to be our therapist based on whether he was a Christian. However, I had heard him give a lecture on the treatment of clients with HIV in which he referenced the importance of respecting clients' religious and spiritual beliefs. Indeed, he was very respectful and affirming of our spiritual beliefs. This was very important to us, because I knew that, at best, many therapists would be doing a great deal of their own internal work, if we were to talk freely about our faith in God. At worst, they would be disrespectful of our beliefs, either overtly or covertly, regardless of whether they were aware of their internal process.

8. Understand that there is no foundation for the dichotomy of spiritual faith versus empirical fact.

Historically, many people have seen religion and science as adversaries. We believe that others have viewed religion and science as unrelated, mutually exclusive competitors in explaining the meaning-making process of life. We acknowledge that some people have chosen science to be their sole religion, and others have chosen religion to be there sole science. We believe that both religion and science provide information that is helpful to the soul. We have heard several people over the years say things such as, "Your opinion is just a matter of faith. I prefer to base my opinions on empirical facts." This underlying assumption of a mutually exclusive dichotomy is being challenged today in many places. Contrary to historical views, "Research suggests that religious faith—whether it's Jewish, Muslim, Catholic, Protestant, Buddhist, or other—may actually enhance mental health, at least in some cases" (Clay, 1996, p. 1).

If a person reads newspapers or magazines, watches news programs on television, or surfs the Web, he or she cannot help but run into stories about scientific research involving religion and/or religious issues. For example, a quick trip to CNN's Web site (www.cnn.com) on February 28, 2002, allowed us to locate a number of interesting articles related to spirituality and health. Titles such as, "Doctors Explore Use of Prayer to Fight Disease," "Study: Religion Helps Smokers Kick the Habit," "Probing the Power of Prayer," and "Spirituality May Help People Live Longer," were listed. These articles reference studies on a variety of topics. For example, one study found that AIDS patients in a prayed-for group lived longer than did patients in a control group (cited in Levine, 1996b). Another study found that " 'Smokers in the intensive spiritually based intervention were three times more likely to make positive progress,' said Carolyn Voorhees of Johns Hopkins Medical Institutions" (Levine, 1996a, pp. 1-2). Another study found that folks "who attended religious services at least once a week" were 46 percent less likely to die during the six-year study (cited in Cutter, 1999, p. 2). In this article, the lead author of this study, Harold Koenig, a psychiatrist at Duke University Medical Center, said, "When we controlled for such things as age, race, how sick they were and other health and social factors, there was still a 28 percent reduction in mortality" (p. 2). Koenig went on to say that the reduction in the mortality rates of regular churchgoers was comparable to that of nonsmokers over smokers.

We could go on and on referencing studies that demonstrated that religious service attendance and/or faith were positively correlated with things such as decreased blood pressure, fewer hospital visits, lower rates of suicide, alcoholism, etc. However, we are very aware of the skeptics who would immediately question the methodology of these specific studies. Although many of these studies have recently been published in respectable journals, such as *The International Journal of Psychiatry Medicine,* the *American Journal of Psychiatry,* and the *Journal of Gerontology: Medical Sciences,* we respect the skeptics' right to question the methodology and/or present alternative reasons for the findings. We have heard some skeptics attribute the positive relationships between prayer and benefits such as reductions in blood pressure and mortality rates to nothing more than the natural by-product of the relaxation and lowered heart rates that can occur during prayer rather than to "a God who answers prayer." This, of course, is a reasonable hypothesis, yet Larry Dossey noted that even rodents heal faster when prayed for (in Levine, 1996b).

However, to respect our skeptical friends and their right to doubt the methodology of single studies, let's take a look at what meta-analyses and extensive literature reviews have shown. Meta-analyses can be used to see whether there are consistent trends across similar studies that used different methodological approaches.

In an attempt to discover whether there was a relationship between religiosity and mental health, Bergin (1983) conducted an extensive meta-analysis on this topic and found essentially no relationship between pathology and religious affiliation. Based on thirty effects from twenty-four studies, 47 percent exhibited a positive relationship between religiousness and mental health, 23 percent suggested a negative relationship, and 30 percent no relationship. Bergin (1983) concludes, "Perhaps the most definitive thing that can be said is that religious phenomena are multidimensional" (p. 179).

In all seven studies reviewed by Larson (1985), a positive relationship existed between self-reported marital satisfaction and church attendance. Also, religious faith and commitment were found to be beneficial for individuals who were coping with the threat of a loss or death (Gorsuch, 1988; McCrae, 1984; Pargament et al., 1992). In an extensive literature review, Levin and Vanderpool (1987) reported that twenty-two out of the twenty-seven studies they reviewed found a significant, positive association between frequency of religious service attendance and physical health.

Gartner (1996) reviewed numerous studies on a variety of different dimensions. A review of nine studies resulted in a strong finding that religiously devoted individuals tend to live longer. Five of the six studies Gartner reviewed demonstrated a negative relationship between depression and religious commitment. Furthermore, every one of the twelve studies he reviewed with regard to suicide revealed a negative relationship between suicide and religiosity. Eleven of the twelve studies reviewed found a negative relationship between drug use and religious commitment. Six of the seven studies reviewed demonstrated that individuals with higher levels of religious commitment were less likely to use or abuse alcohol. Gartner also discovered that that there were negative relationships between religious service attendance and delinquency in twelve of the thirteen studies he reviewed. A negative relationship between divorce and church attendance was found in every one of the five studies reviewed.

In summary, although no causal relationships have been demonstrated, religious service attendance and/or faith positively affected physical health, life longevity, effectiveness of coping, and marital satisfaction. Also, religious service attendance and/or faith lowered the rate of depression, suicide, drug use, alcohol abuse, delinquency, and divorce.

Skeptics will be pleased to note that Gartner (1996) suggested that physical health may elevate religious service attendance rather than vice versa. In fact, some might even go so far as to suggest that all of this research could be explained by the fact that people who attend church are able to because they are physically healthy, and because they are physically healthy, they are in better spirits. They might even point out that "Even you admitted that no causal relationships have been demonstrated."

Therefore, let us look at a study conducted by Randolph Byrd that was published in the *Southern Medical Journal* in 1988. Byrd conducted a study over ten months in which 393 patients, who were admitted to the coronary care unit of San Francisco General Medical Center, were randomly assigned to one of two groups. Approximately half of the patients (201 patients) were assigned to a control group and were given state-of-the-art treatment. The other half (192 patients) were assigned to an intercessory prayer group and were given the same state-of-the-art care but were also prayed for by Christian prayer groups throughout the United States. This study was a prospective randomized double-blind study. In other words, methodologically speaking, it doesn't get any better than this. None of the patients, nurses, and doctors knew which patients were being prayed for. Results demonstrated that the prayed-for patients had fewer deaths, experienced less pulmonary edema (lungs filling with fluid), required less ventilatory assistance, fewer antibiotics, and fewer diuretics than did the patients in the control group. In commenting on this study, Larry Dossey said, "The outcome was so significant that if the method being investigated had been a new drug or surgical technique, it would undoubtedly have been heralded as a scientific breakthrough" (p. 1).

A more recent study on cardiac care patients that used similar methodology, conducted by a research team headed by William Harris, also found that patients in a prayed-for group fared significantly better than did patients in the control group. This study was published in the October 25, 1999, issue of the *Archives of Internal Medicine* (cited in Rauch, 2000).

Regardless of what research studies have found, we have no doubt that some skeptics still remain. We cannot convince you to believe that which you choose not to believe, and can only control what we can control. Of course, we believe that the empirical evidence regarding some of the benefits of spiritual faith is overwhelming. However, we understand that some will doubt the findings from specific studies, literature reviews of empirical studies, meta-analyses, and randomized double-blind studies. We respect your right to doubt infinitem. However, we would simply caution you to be careful. In the words of C. S. Lewis ([1947] 1996),

> But you cannot go on "explaining away" forever: you will find that you have explained explanation itself away. (p. 86)

9. Be willing to question your client's spiritual beliefs.

The idea here is to remain curious so you can learn about your client's unique beliefs. Again, this isn't really anything we therapists do not do in other realms of our work. Questions such as, "Please tell me more about how this belief influences your views in this area of your life?" and "Would you please tell me more about what you believe it is that God wants you to do in this instance?" are types of questions that therapists would normally feel very free to ask, if the discussion were focused on a topic other than spirituality. For example, would a therapist think twice about asking a question such as, "Please tell me more about how your views of marriage influence you in your dating relationships?" How about, "Would you please tell me more about what you believe it is that your mother would have wanted you to do in this instance?" Why is it that many therapists think they can't ask a client questions about a topic that the client likely introduced anyway? No doubt, these therapists feel the power of spirituality. We are simply encouraging therapists to see this power as a potential ally when working with their clients rather than subconsciously allowing their own fear to give them messages that lead them to believe they can't ask a client questions about their beliefs. You're unlikely to get "snake bit" if you ask a client about his or her beliefs.

I (PK) worked with a client recently, Edward, who reported that he was confronted with a career decision because he had experienced some unexpected health problems. Edward responded very well to the overture, "Help me to understand your world and/or life view in relation to the challenges you are facing." Edward reported that he was a Buddhist and said that he believed some challenges in life are presented to people to help them reach a higher level. He also said that he believes that everyone has "God within" them and that people can get in the way of this divinity being actualized; hence, problems can result from this. After listening to Edward beat up on himself for a while, due to the challenges he was facing, I asked him a question based on some of the spiritual beliefs he had espoused. "How would you be able to differentiate between whether this challenge in your life is a blessing, perhaps placed in your life path to help you grow or whether this challenge is a problem that you have brought on yourself?" Edward reported that he hadn't thought of his career decision as a potential opportunity, but, instead, had assumed that it was a problem that he had brought on himself.

By remaining curious and asking Edward questions about his own beliefs, I was able to help him clearly see some of the issues that were contributing to the cognitive dissonance and confusion he was experiencing. In fact, at the end of this particular session, Edward told me, "I hope you don't take this in a wrong fashion, but I can clearly see God working through you. I believe that your depth in understanding spiritual issues in therapy is the difference between you being a mediocre therapist and you being a great therapist." Again, this highlights the importance of remaining curious, demonstrating an ability to respectfully listen to a client's beliefs, even if you don't hold the same religious beliefs, and a willingness to respectfully question clients about their beliefs.

10. Be willing to challenge your client about his or her spiritual beliefs.

Yes, we mean this. Let's acknowledge up front that there's a greater likelihood that more therapists do this poorly than do it in an effective manner. However, that doesn't lead us to conclude, "Therefore, we must not do this at all." We don't do this often. Indeed, if this type of challenge were shown on television there might well be a disclaimer at the bottom that would say, "These are professionals doing this. Please don't try this at home."

Our general rule of thumb is to ask, "Is the client being consistent with his or her espoused beliefs?" not "Is the client being consistent with our beliefs?" For example, I (JR) was working with a young man, Ryan, who reported that he was dealing with some depressive symptoms and some feelings of guilt because he was engaging in premarital sex with his girlfriend. Ryan reported that he was a "strong Christian." In response to the miracle question, "If you were to wake up tomorrow and everything was exactly the way you wanted it to be, what would be different?" Ryan answered that he'd be out of the relationship and would not be having intercourse with his girlfriend. I asked him, "Why do you think you're having sex with her if you don't want to?" Ryan responded, "Well, she made a good point. She told me, 'As a Christian, you believe that you shouldn't judge others or you, too, will be judged. Well, I have sexual needs that I need to get met, and I feel like you are judging me that I'm bad simply because I have these needs. I don't think that's very Christian of you. Aren't you supposed to love me unconditionally?' "

So Ryan reported that he was having intercourse with his girlfriend because he thought that it was his judge-free responsibility as a Christian to have intercourse with her. However, he also reported a belief that, "Based on the Bible, I know that it's against God's plan for me to have intercourse outside of marriage." I questioned him about his beliefs further and respectfully challenged him to explore his beliefs on this subject in greater depth. I asked, "I'm a little confused. Can you help me understand in greater depth why it is that you believe God wants you to do something that you believe God doesn't want you to do?" Ryan said, "Yeah, it's kind of screwed up, isn't it?" I then asked Ryan if he had ever heard of the concept of competing needs. He said that he hadn't, and asked me what it meant. I explained that sometimes a person has needs that are in direct opposition to what another person's needs are. In such instances, there isn't a middle ground because the needs are mutually exclusive. By the very nature of the situation, if one person's need gets met, the other person's need cannot be met. So, either one person must give in and not get his or her need met, or conflict will eventually occur. However, I also explained that if a person's need touches on his or her convictions, often the person who gives in can grow to resent the partner and/or even himself or herself because there is no sense of peace about the unmet need. Therefore, sometimes giving in on certain issues can unintentionally lead to further difficulties in relationships. Ryan thanked me for explaining this concept to him and told me that he felt somewhat relieved to find out that he didn't have to always sacrifice his needs in a relationship to be a good partner. I affirmed his conclusion. Eventually, Ryan made positive strides toward successfully reaching his espoused goals.

Another example of an instance in which we might challenge our client's beliefs would be if a client espoused religious beliefs that suggested that he or she should commit suicide or sexually abuse a child. These instances are the reason we place the word *general* before our previously mentioned rule of thumb. Although it has been our experience that this very rarely happens, we can set our watches to questions containing scenarios such as this being posed to us in our seminars. It's almost as if the fear that this could happen, which we acknowledge it could, paralyzes therapists, leading them to justify their learned avoidance with regard to addressing spiritual issues in therapy. Clearly, there are times in therapy when respect for the client as a human being must take precedence over respect for his or her espoused beliefs. We understand that the client can hold such a belief. We, as therapists, are simply forced to recognize the consequences of the client holding such beliefs and must take the appropriate ethical and legal steps that are needed. However, we don't believe that this is not respecting the client. Instead, we believe that we are truly respecting the person of the client.

FROM SUICIDAL PSYCHOSIS TO SACRED SLEEP

I (PK) was working in a psychiatric emergency room several years ago when I had an interesting encounter with a patient. One of the attending physicians came into the pit and commented, "The paranoid schizophrenic in room two is fighting against the effects of the Haldol. I've tried everything, but she keeps claiming that God doesn't want her to sleep. She hasn't slept or eaten in over forty-eight hours." About thirty minutes later, the pit boss asked me to go check on this patient, Shannon. So, I went into room two, quite scared, I might add, since I had not worked in this environment very long.

In the room, I found Shannon walking back and forth using her fingers to hold her eyes wide open. I asked Shannon how she was doing. She said, "God told me to kill myself."

Surprised, yet trying to stay present with her, I asked, "How did God relay this message to you?"

Shannon said, "He told me to kill myself right after Satan told me to kill myself."

I asked, "You could actually hear their voices?"

Shannon responded, "Yes. They talk to me quite a bit."

Not having a clue where to go with this information, I defaulted to a question and asked her, "How do you tell the difference between God's voice and Satan's voice?"

"I don't know. Sometimes I can't."

Sensing a possible opening I asked, "Then how can you be absolutely certain that it wasn't just Satan who told you to kill yourself?"

Shannon responded, "You're right. I guess I can't."

Full of much more hope than knowledge and noticing the tray of untouched food on the desk in the room, I then asked her, "When was the last time you ate any food?"

"Three days ago."

"Wow, you must be hungry," I replied.

"But God told me not to eat anything."

"Are you sure it was God, or could it have been Satan?"

She said, "That's a good question."

"Shannon, has God ever told you anything about the importance of taking care of your body?"

"Yes."

"Where was that?"

"In the Bible," she said.

"Do you believe in the Bible?"

"Oh, yes I do! I'm a Christian."

"Yeah, me too," I replied. "I seem to remember that somewhere in the Bible God says that our body is a temple and we're supposed to take care of it. Do you remember that?"

Shannon said enthusiastically, "Yes, I remember that."

Then, getting more hopeful and relaxed, I said, "Do you think that God thinks that eating a balanced diet and getting good sleep is better or worse for our temple than is not eating or sleeping at all?"

"I bet it's better for us to eat and sleep," Shannon responded.

"I agree with you. You think it might be OK with God if you ate something that would be good for your temple?"

"Yes," she said, as she picked up a roll from the tray and began to eat.

"Shannon, I'm going to let you eat and nourish your temple, but I'll be back to check on you in a little bit." She said that was OK. About fifteen minutes later, one of the attending physicians came in the pit, where I was doing some paperwork, and said, "Look at Shannon. What happened to her?" I looked up and she was lying down on a couch in the common area sleeping very soundly.

Although we don't believe that integrating spiritual conversations in the treatment of all patients or clients will be helpful, we also don't believe we have to avoid talking about spirituality simply because a person is challenged with psychoses. We've heard some professionals erroneously assert that if a client is psychotic and is talking about religious faith, the person, therefore, must have a psychotic type of faith. Certainly, this pathway may not work with all patients diagnosed with schizophrenia. However, for Shannon, including her spiritual faith in our conversation created an avenue for her to explore alternative messages from God, without having to leave her own espoused faith base. If she had not said that she believed in the Bible, I would not have taken the direction that I did with my questioning. However, remaining curious through the art of questioning provided a pathway for me to challenge Shannon's assumptions about the voice of God by simply using her espoused spiritual beliefs as a foundation for such a challenge. Again, our general rule of thumb that I followed in this real-life example helped Shannon to get some very much needed sleep and nutrition. Ask yourself whether the client is being consistent with his or her espoused beliefs, not whether the client is being consistent with your beliefs.

SUMMARY

We make no claims that this is an all-inclusive, exhaustive list of ways therapists can help support the spiritual health of their clients in therapy. In fact, there are many other helpful ways therapists can work with their clients and approach therapeutic discussions involving spiritual issues. We hope these ten ways therapists can help support the spiritual health of their clients will be a starting point for you to think about other ways you could help some of your clients feel free to be authentic about who they are as spiritual beings. For it is a fact that the power of spirituality in therapy can be very helpful to the therapeutic process. However, it's also a fact that the power of spirituality in therapy can be approached in ways that are very harmful to clients and the therapeutic process.

Chapter 13

The Power to Hurt

The concept of power, whether of a god or of a man, always includes the ability to help and the ability to harm.

Friedrich Nietzsche
The Will to Power

We believe that one of the biggest reasons why the integration of spirituality, religion, and psychotherapy has been so widely debated over the course of history is because people have often fallen into the trap of seeing the issue as a dichotomy. "Are you pro-integration or anti-integration?" This type of debate within our field has not been confined to the realm of spirituality and psychotherapy. In fact, there's a long history of this type of debate in many areas. How short would introductory textbooks in psychology be if there was never a nature versus nurture debate? How long did it take for someone with enough intellect and grace to suggest, "Perhaps human beings are influenced by both nature and nurturance"? This both/and type of thinking often comes in handy when introducing healthy change at a process level when people have become polarized due to either/or type thinking at a content level. Indeed, spirituality can be a powerfully helpful source of influence in therapy, but it can also be a powerfully harmful source.

TWO VIGNETTES

We illustrate this point further with two vignettes that exemplify two of the ways that therapists can practice spiritually incompetent therapy. In each vignette, a spiritually incompetent therapist will be working with a married, heterosexual couple on issues related to their marriage.

Role-Play #1: The Active Avoider

DR. GODCRUTCH: Welcome. What is it that I can help you with?

JOE: Well, doctor, my wife and I are having some challenges in our relationship.

MARY: Yes, since the time our daughter was diagnosed with cancer, it seems like we get irritated with each other quite a bit. It almost seems as if we can't please each other sometimes.

DR. GODCRUTCH: I'm sorry to hear about your daughter's cancer. Mary, you mentioned that at times it seems like neither of you can please the other. You're suggesting that this is not always the case. Could you tell me what has been helpful for you both when you do please each other?

MARY: Well, our church has been very helpful.

JOE: Yes. Our pastor has visited us at the hospital and others have been very supportive as well.

DR. GODCRUTCH: What else has been helpful?

JOE: Well, it seems that whenever we pray together, things usually feel better between us.

MARY: Yes, that's true. Prayer seems to be very helpful and comforting.

DR. GODCRUTCH: Is there anything else that's been helpful?

MARY: Our faith in God has been very helpful. You see, our daughter has a type of cancer that is terminal. Her oncologist has advised us that she may not have more than three weeks to live. Obviously, this is difficult for us to hear, yet we believe God will help us get through this.

JOE: I agree with Mary. Although it doesn't take the pain away, it's helpful to know that our daughter will be in heaven with Jesus when she dies.

DR. GODCRUTCH: I see. [Long pause.] Is there anything concrete that you have done to try to help your marriage during this time?

MARY: Yes, we've read scripture verses together in the morning. We've found this to be very comforting.

JOE: Yes, that's helped a great deal.

DR. GODCRUTCH: What I'm looking for is . . . something other than religion. Have you done anything outside of religion to help you during these times?

JOE: I'm not exactly sure what you're trying to suggest. You have to understand that our faith in God is the most important thing in our lives.

DR. GODCRUTCH: Ahh! Have you ever considered that this might be part of your problem?

MARY: What?

JOE: Do what?

DR. GODCRUTCH: What I mean is that this religiospiritual type of talk seems to be so pervasive that it has inundated your thought processes with illusions of grandeur in the form of a pie in the sky. Perhaps you and your family would be better off if you were to confront your defense mechanisms directly and take a more realistic perspective toward life. Perhaps you should . . . What? What are you doing? Where are you going?

JOE AND MARY: [Exit the therapy room visibly disgusted and shaking their heads.]

Role-Play #2: The Active Proselytizer

DR. MYWAY: Welcome. How may I be helpful to you both today?

RACHEL: Well, doctor, we're having some problems in our marriage.

JAKE: Yes, we're arguing almost every day.

DR. MYWAY: What is it that you typically argue about?

RACHEL: My husband doesn't do any of the work at home. I'm home all day taking care of our three children, all under the age of four, plus cooking and cleaning . . . and he won't help at all.

JAKE: It's not that I won't help at all, I believe that I am helping. I'm working almost sixty hours per week and I get tired. When I come home I just want to relax, but she thinks I'm lazy. I'm not lazy. She just can't relate to me because she doesn't work.

RACHEL: I don't work? I work twenty-four hours a day, seven days a week! When do I get to relax?

DR. MYWAY: Is this the type of conversation that goes on at home?

RACHEL: Yes!

JAKE: You betcha!

DR. MYWAY: We often run into problems in marriages because we have different expectations of what marriage is all about. Rachel, what were your expectations about being a wife of noble character?

RACHEL: I believe that it's my responsibility to be the best mother and wife I can be. I don't mind doing most of the housework, but it would be nice if he would help me every once in a while. He takes me for granted. He doesn't appreciate what I do in our family. I feel like he doesn't respect me.

DR. MYWAY: Did you talk about your expectations for marriage with your pastor when you went through premarital counseling?

RACHEL: No.

JAKE: No, we don't have a pastor.

DR. MYWAY: I'm sorry, I assumed you were Protestant. Have you ever talked about this with a priest?

RACHEL [Looking at Jake in a confused manner]: No.

JAKE: Dr. Myway, we don't have a priest either.

DR. MYWAY: Well, maybe the lack of spirituality in your life is contributing to your problems, but this is something we can work on. This reminds me of something that Jesus once said [leaning over he picks up a Bible and starts thumbing through it]. I think it was in Mark where he said . . .

JAKE: [interrupting Dr. Myway] Doctor, we are Jewish!

DR. MYWAY: [Briefly pausing as he's holding the Bible] That's OK. Jesus was Jewish, too. Hold on just one second. Yes, it was in Mark where he said . . . Hold on. What are you doing? Where are you going? I found it! Come back.

JAKE AND RACHEL: [They both get up and leave the room shaking their heads in disgust.]

We hope that these vignettes will help to increase your awareness of some of the ways that therapists can mishandle conversations of spirituality in therapy. Although we are aware that the therapists' mistakes are quite apparent in these vignettes, we think they both illustrate how therapists can ineffectively address spiritual issues in therapy in potentially harmful ways. As shown, there is more than one way in which therapists can get in the way of clients who are sharing their unique stories in therapy. Perhaps we can all agree that there is no therapeutic justice in cases such as these.

> Justice, then, is when clients can tell their stories as they experience them, the only just censorship being that of protecting others from harm. The space that this justice would create for clients to speak of their experiences with a personal God can be limited both by proscriptive constraints—that this God-talk is not to be spoken of here, and by prescriptive constraints—that God can and should be spoken of here, but only in a certain way. (Griffith, 1995b, p. 124)

We've talked quite extensively about proscriptive constraints by addressing the factors related to learned avoidance, aspiritualism, and the pink elephant in the ivory tower. We also trust that Dr. Godcrutch will leave quite an impression on you. Therefore, we've chosen to address, in greater depth, issues related to prescriptive constraints. We've also chosen to address some very subtle prescriptive constraints as well as more easily recognizable ones. Regardless, we hope you'll find these discussions thought-provoking. Rather than seeing this list as complete, we hope you'll join us in seeing it as the beginning point of the conversation. With that in mind, we offer the following ten principles, in no particular order of significance, as things that therapists can do to practice spiritually incompetent therapy.

TEN WAYS THERAPISTS CAN HARM SPIRITUAL HEALTH IN THERAPY

1. Believe, "Since I am a therapist and I believe in God, I am automatically effective at integrating spirituality and therapy."

This is a common mistake. A person can see some of the possible results of such thinking in the example of the vignette of Dr. Myway. Sometimes people can have such powerful and life-changing spiritual experiences that they want others to experience the same thing. Although we appreciate the good intentions of such well-meaning therapists, we wonder if their own positive experience(s) resulted from someone else mandating that they have such an experience? Our guess would be it wasn't. Regardless of whether it's a spiritual issue, an overzealous therapist is a potential source of harm to the client and the therapeutic process.

A pseudoconverse of this assumption is also quite common. "Since I don't believe in God, I can't talk about a client's spirituality in therapy." This type of thinking was demonstrated in our previous discussion of the practicum supervisor who deferred to the Christian student to give advice to one of his classmates who was working with a client who was a professing Christian. Again, a person doesn't have to reinvent the wheel to grasp this concept. How often do therapists think, "Since I haven't had a sexual dysfunction, I can't talk about them when working with an individual who is experiencing sexual problems," or "Since I've never had major depression, I can't work with a person who is dealing with depressive symptoms"?

We'd like to comment that this work is often not easy. However, since we have discovered that neither avoiding nor ignoring are healthy alternatives, perhaps a referral to another therapist with expertise in this area would be the best option in certain cases. In some instances, we believe that a referral would be the best option. For example, it would be very challenging for a therapist who believes that God is only an illusion to work with a person who strongly believes in the reality of God and the power of God in his or her life. The operative question is, "Could he or she do it well at all?" Again, we hope that no one is offended by our position on this issue, but we really don't think this is rocket science either.

Noted social scientist Harry Callahan (character played by Clint Eastwood in *Magnum Force* [1973]), once said, "A man's got to know his limitations." So, we'll acknowledge our limitations along a similar dimension. We'd be extremely challenged if we were working with a client who wanted us to help him or her find a way to reach his or her therapeutic goal, moving closer to the Widgetmaker of Widgetville. Although we could be empathic with the client through understanding that he or she really believed in Widgetville, if we thought it was an illusion, would we really be the best therapists to help the client reach Widgetville? We think not. In fact, our belief in the nonexistence of Widgetville would likely influence us to assess for possible psychosis. Therefore, perhaps the best way that some therapists can effectively integrate spirituality and therapy is to refer spiritual clients to a therapist who is able and willing to effectively do so.

2. Debate doctrine and/or theology (point based on Bergin, Payne, and Richards, 1996).

Short and sweet, ask yourself the following two questions: "What is my motivation in doing this?" and "How will this be helpful?" We love to debate theology and discuss religious differences in our spare time. However, we believe that getting into debates over theological issues with our clients would be inappropriate and harmful to the therapeutic relationship. A person can enjoy debating doctrine and theology and still be a therapist; just leave the debate outside of the therapy room.

3. Assume, "Since my client is a member of the same religion that I am, we share the same spiritual beliefs" (point based on Wulff, 1996).

The astute reader will remember that sharing the same spiritual beliefs as a client was also on the list of ways that therapists could help spiritual health in therapy. Although we do believe there are some benefits of having a therapist and clients share similar religious beliefs, we also believe that this can lead to the development of erroneous assumptions that could be harmful to the therapeutic process. For example, imagine the awkwardness in the following minivignette we call "open mouth, insert foot therapy":

CLIENT: I went to church this week and it was very comforting to me. Personally, there's nothing like going to a traditional, liturgical Lutheran service and worshiping God with like-minded people. I struggle with some of the far-out beliefs of other denominations that present themselves as progressive.

THERAPIST: Yes, I know what you mean. I'm Lutheran as well and I have a hard time with some of these churches who are ordaining women as pastors.

CLIENT: Oh, you must be a member of a different denomination. I wasn't talking about that type of thing. In fact, my sister is the pastor at my ELCA [Evangelical Lutheran Church in America] church.

Be aware that self-identification as a member of a particular religion will not always inform you as to what religious and/or spiritual beliefs a client may hold. I (Peter) was reminded of this recently when a colleague of mine referred to himself as a Christian, and then informed me that he disagreed with most of Jesus' teachings and did not think that Jesus was truly the Messiah. In fact, he even, in a subtle manner, poked fun at Christians who believed that Jesus is God. (I should not have been surprised by this statement, for this was the same colleague who had previously told me that he believed in an omniscient God who did not know everything. Limited omniscience? There's a concept to ponder, but I've digressed.) I must admit that I was glad he was a colleague and not one of my clients. This enabled me to join him in the fun that he was obviously having. I proceeded to inform him that I was a Freudian, but then told him that I rejected all of Freud's teachings. Slow to the punch, my colleague asked, "How then can you call yourself a Freudian?" I simply responded, "Let not your question go unexamined by you, for this is analogous to your self-identification as a Christian." This statement is in accord with the following explanation by G. K. Chesterton ([1908] 1995):

> In one sense, of course, all intelligent ideas are narrow. They cannot be broader than themselves. A Christian is only restricted in the same sense that an atheist is restricted. He cannot think Christianity false and continue to be a Christian; and the atheist cannot think atheism false and continue to be an atheist. (p. 28)

In summary, guard against acting on assumptions based solely on religious labels espoused by clients who have not yet espoused specific spiritual and/or religious beliefs. And even then, remain curious.

4. Do not remain curious of a client's beliefs.

Although we realize we've already addressed this concept, we believe this is such a key concept that, even though it is interrelated with many of the issues we have and will discuss, it deserves a space of its own. Melissa Elliott refers to a concept she calls "the entrapment of knowing." The idea is that once therapists believe they know something for certain, they lose curiosity around this topic. This assumed certainty can potentially lead therapists into mistake-making in therapy due to the erroneous assumptions that result from knowing all there is to know around a certain topic. Rather than taking a posture of certainty, the therapist is encouraged to remain curious around the issues that his or her clients are presenting with in therapy. This posture of curiosity provides therapists and clients with the freedom of maneuverability to continue to explore and to learn from each other. Curiosity also connotes interest. If the therapist respectfully remains curious about a client's spiritual and/or religious beliefs, the client will generally feel more freedom to share the things that are important to his or her life. When curiosity ends, the therapist can quickly fall into the trap of believing he or she knows all he or she needs to know about a client's situation. This type of mistake can lead a therapist to act on this assumption and potentially believe something to be true that indeed is not.

Indiscriminate Discrimination

I (Peter) once worked with a client, Kelly, who told me that she was reluctant to enter into therapy because of an experience she had with a previous therapist. She told me that she was happily married with two young children. Kelly reported that she had entered therapy the previous year because she had discovered that she was attracted to women and was hoping to gain some sense of peace about these feelings. She told me that she had stopped going to therapy with her previous therapist because, after she told him her story, he told her that these feelings were likely an indication that she was a lesbian. Kelly reported that this therapist suggested she should not be alarmed and that it was common to be scared during the initial phase of discovering that one is gay. During this session, he reportedly told her that even though it would likely be difficult for her to come out because of her family situation, it would probably be best for her in the long run.

Kelly told me that she was very much in love with her husband and would not do anything to risk damaging her marriage. She reported that she was hoping to be able to talk about the influence these thoughts and feelings were having on her life as a married woman, not to have a therapist tell her that she was a lesbian who needed to come out. Kelly went on to report that she was a Christian and was hurt and offended that a therapist would suggest that she needed to do something that was against her spiritual beliefs and was inconsistent with her reported goals for therapy.

This case is an excellent example of how important it is for therapists to remain curious when working with their clients. It also raises some provocative questions. As most therapists know, conversion therapy is a very hot topic in our field today. In a nutshell, conversion therapy is a type of therapy in which the therapeutic goal is to help clients who have reported homosexual feelings embrace a heterosexual lifestyle. Indeed, this is a controversial practice that has received a great deal of attention from the American Psychological Association in recent years. In fact the American Psychological Association (1998) has taken the stance that it is unethical to practice conversion therapy. Regardless of whether you agree with the American Psychological Association's position on this issue, we don't think it really matters for the sake of this discussion. We would simply like to pose some questions for you to consider.

- Is it possible for individuals to be attracted to people of their same gender and not be gay?
- Considering that the bisexual community has talked about being discriminated against by both the heterosexual and homosexual communities, is it wise for any therapist to dichotomize sexual orientation?
- If a client has homosexual feelings but reports that he or she does not want to act on them because of his or her religious beliefs, how would you approach such a client? Would you respect your client's right to spiritual autonomy or would you believe it was your responsibility as the therapist to educate this client that this is a common challenge for all members of the gay, lesbian, and bisexual (GLB) community who grow up in a "heterosexist religion"?
- Is it possible that the therapist in the previous example could have, perhaps unknowingly and unintentionally, practiced another form of conversion therapy?

Indeed, these are some difficult questions to address. However, we believe it's imperative for all therapists to honestly address questions such as these in a proactive manner. If not, they'll likely end up flying by the seat of their pants and reacting to these issues when they arise in therapy based on their own unexplored blind spots. Again, regardless of how you responded to the previous questions, we trust that you'll agree with us that it would be wise for therapists to address their true beliefs on these topics so they can hopefully avoid falling prey to the assumption of unidirectional conversion therapy. Indeed, Kelly's therapist could have benefited from remaining curious about Kelly's spiritual beliefs and therapeutic goals rather than psychoeducationally instructing her that she would benefit from coming out.

5. Position yourself, and/or be ignorant that your client has positioned himself or herself, as spiritually one-up (point based on Rotz, Russel, and Wright, 1993).

This is a potentially dangerous dynamic that the competent therapist would be wise to be aware of and avoid if at all possible. Whether or not the thought is overtly articulated in therapy, taking a position that, "Regardless of what you may believe, I know better than you do what you need to do," is a potentially dangerous position for the therapist to take. In fact, sometimes the therapist may believe that something else may likely be more helpful for the client than the current path he or she is taking. However, even in these instances, any thought that would begin with "Regardless of what you may believe . . ." seems to suggest some spiritual narcissism on the part of the therapist. The therapist would be wise to remain curious about his or her client's beliefs as well as remaining curious about the potential influence that his or her own beliefs could have on the therapeutic process.

Clients are not immune from taking on this one-up role either. For example, most of our clients who come into couple therapy are experts about what their partner needs to do differently. Some clients are often not as skilled at looking into the mirror as they are at trying to be the mirror that their partner needs to look into. This dynamic is definitely not extinct within the spiritual realm either. If a therapist is not careful, the clients may have some success getting the therapist to collude with their position about what their partner needs to do differently, regardless of whether the therapist is aware of this process. For example, "Doctor, as a man of faith yourself, you'll understand that I struggle with the fact that my husband is not taking the role of the spiritual leader in our household. Can you help him to understand the importance of this from a spiritual perspective?" Or "Doc, the problem here is that my wife is not being submissive to me like the good book says. Can you help me to understand how I'm supposed to act when she's walking counter to the word?" Of course, a pseudoconverse of this example could also be problematic. For example, "Doctor, I fully understand that my wife is a religious person and I can support that. However, although I went to church when I was younger and naive, I no longer need the type of help that my wife needs. Can you help her to understand that I've advanced beyond this point?" Buy into these types of "invitations" as they are phrased when working with individuals, couples, and families in therapy, and you'll soon find that you've lost a great deal of power to be a helpful therapist for your clients.

6. Claim and/or believe that you have divine knowledge.

We were at a state conference some years ago where two therapists were conducting a workshop on their particular counseling approach as Christian therapists working with Christian clients. We found that these therapists had some good things to say, yet we were very uncomfortable with some of the things they presented. During one part of their presentation, they asked for a volunteer from the audience to participate in a live example of the type of work they do with their clients. A brave audience member volunteered and agreed to take part in this part of their presentation.

During their interview with the woman who volunteered, she reported that she was dealing with some challenges in her life related to loneliness. She reported that she was single but wished she could find a male partner with whom she could have a healthy relationship. She reported that she had been involved in dating relationships in the past but was disappointed that for one reason or another they just never seemed to work out. She reported that she even questioned whether a man would find her attractive in the future. She said that she believed and trusted in God, but sometimes wondered whether it was in His future plans for her to have a healthy romantic relationship. Then the interviewer suggested they take a break from their conversation and turned toward the audience so she could articulate how she was conceptualizing this case.

One of the presenters then said something such as, "See, the problem in this case is that she doesn't have strong enough faith. The loneliness and lack of confidence in the future suggests that the client could benefit from stronger faith. So, our work will center on helping to strengthen this client's faith." Our jaws dropped. We were amazed that these therapists had essentially said, in front of this woman, that everything in her life would be better if she just had stronger faith in God.

It's indeed a difficult challenge to do live work in front of other people. However, with this difficult challenge also comes responsibility. We don't believe the therapists had nearly enough information to challenge this woman's faith, let alone to attribute her difficulties in life to this lack of faith. For if all challenges in the lives of Christians are due to a lack of faith in God, Christians are left to answer many questions about the lives of Job and Jesus, just to name two. To enter into conversations about faith, spirituality, and/or God necessitates humility. To speak about God is not the same as to speak for God. Indeed, God may use therapists to help clients. However, therapists who assume that God *is* using them as an agent for change right now simultaneously assume that God is certainly using them now, and in so doing they negate the possibility that God may simply be using them to help prepare the client for future change. Simply acknowledging that God is a part of the equation does not eliminate the risk of therapists unknowingly placing themselves in the role of an all-knowing being. It's best to remain a therapist and to let God be God.

> *For whoever exalts himself will be humbled, and whoever humbles himself will be exalted.*
>
> Jesus, Matthew 23:12

7. Try to rescue God.

On more than one occasion, we've seen therapists become uncomfortable with how a client is speaking of God during a therapeutic conversation. Indeed, some therapists become uncomfortable with any type of God talk. However, what we're focusing on in this example is when a therapist, who is often a spiritual person, becomes uncomfortable when a client talks about God in a way that threatens the therapist's view of God. One of our colleagues even said, "I've feared becoming collateral damage if the proverbial lightning bolt should strike my client." Let's illustrate this point further through another self-reflexive exercise.

Self-Reflexercise

Read the following quotation and imagine that these are the words of a client with whom you're currently working. Pay particular attention to your own reaction, thoughts, and feelings as you read the words.

> And no one ever told me about the laziness of grief. Except at my job—where the machine seems to run on much as usual—I loathe the slightest effort. Not only writing but even reading a letter is too much. Even shaving. What does it matter now whether my cheek is rough or smooth? They say an unhappy man wants distractions—something to take him out of himself. Only as a dog-tired man wants an extra blanket on a cold night; he'd rather lie there shivering than get up and find one. It's easy to see why the lonely become untidy; finally, dirty and disgusting . . .

What types of issues might this client be dealing with? What possible psychological issues and/or symptoms do you hear in the words spoken by this client? Now, the client continues.

> Meanwhile, where is God? This is one of the most disquieting symptoms. When you are happy, so happy that you have no sense of needing Him, so happy that you are tempted to feel His claims upon you as an interruption, if you remember yourself and turn to Him with gratitude and praise, you will be—or so it feels—welcomed with open arms. But go to Him when your need is desperate, when all other help is vain, and what do you find? A door slammed in your face, and a sound of bolting and double bolting on the inside. After that, silence. You may as well turn away. The longer you wait, the more emphatic the silence will become.

What types of thoughts are going through your mind with regard to this client? What types of assumptions do you have about this client's faith in God? Do you think this client needs stronger faith? What if you found out that this client was living with his brother, who, at times, has struggled with alcohol abuse? What if you found out that this client's mother had died many years earlier from cancer? What if you found out that this was an excerpt from your client's journal? What if you found out that this client's wife had just recently died of cancer? What if you found out that this client was a professor at one of the most prestigious universities in the world? What if you found out that his name is C. S. Lewis (1963, p. 17-18), one of the most, if not the most, highly respected Christian apologists of the twentieth century?

It's so important to learn the context in which your clients live. We've seen therapists give their clients pep talks in therapy, trying to convince them that things really aren't as bad as they may seem. A therapist might be tempted to say things such as, "But God is there" or "You just need to strengthen your faith." We believe that verbal interventions such as these say a great deal more about where the therapists are with their own issues than they do about where the clients are with theirs.

God doesn't need to be rescued. In fact, we believe that it's better for clients to be authentic with their thoughts toward God rather than sugarcoating their true thoughts and feelings toward Him. We can't tell you how many times we've heard clients say things such as, "I know it is wrong to question God, but . . ." Clients are often already dealing with their own confusion and guilt related to questioning God, doubting God, and even being angry with God. From our spiritual perspective, we believe that God would prefer to have an honest relationship with an angry client, whom He already knows is angry with Him, more than He would an inauthentic relationship with an angry client who feels that he or she must hide his or her true feelings toward God.

"Mere Authenticity"

We've heard clients say, "But I'm not being a good Christian if I question God." I (Peter) once worked with a woman who self-identified as a Christian. Joy was grieving the loss of her husband, who had died after a long battle with cancer. She was trying to present a positive and upbeat picture to her family and friends, but down deep she was really hurting. It took Joy a couple of sessions before she was able to honestly admit that she was extremely sad. I asked her what other emotions she was experiencing. She hesitated, but then she said, "Anger."

"Where is the anger directed?" I asked her.

Joy hesitated again before responding: "It's at God, but I know that this is wrong."

"What is it that you think that is wrong about expressing your anger toward God?"

"I can't get angry with God, it's just not right," she replied.

In the past, Joy had commented that God was the major source of help for her as she was coping with the possible loss of her husband. Remembering how often she would comment about how helpful her prayer life was, I asked her, "Have you told God that you're not allowing yourself to get angry with Him?"

Joy responded, "No."

"May I ask you why you haven't told Him this?"

"I haven't talked with God in well over a week. I haven't felt like I could, because I knew that I was doing something wrong in questioning him," she said.

"OK, that makes sense. Joy, where did you get the idea that it was wrong to question God?"

She hesitated and responded, "I'm not sure where I got that message."

"What if the message that it's wrong to question God is wrong?"

She smiled and said, "That's an interesting thought."

"Where do you think we might be able to find out whether that message is correct?"

"The Bible, of course," she said.

"I agree with you. That sounds like a good place to look. Joy, do you ever remember hearing the words, 'My God, my God. Why have you forsaken me?'"

"Yes, that's what Jesus said on the cross right before he died."

"Yes, you're right, and King David also said the same thing [Psalm 22:1]. Do you believe that Jesus was wrong when he said this?"

"No, Jesus did not sin," she replied.

"Joy, if Jesus was without sin, then it must mean that it isn't necessarily a sin to question God, right?"

She smiled and said, "You're right. I never thought of it that way before." The next week, Joy reported that she was feeling quite a bit better after spending a great deal of time in prayer, getting her thoughts and feelings off of her chest.

Some might suggest, "But you just imposed your beliefs onto the client." Perhaps a person could make that argument. We would simply say that if taking a position, based on the client's own reported beliefs in God, that helps a client connect with the most important source of help in his or her support system is wrong, then we are guilty as charged. We would not do this with every client. We would not even necessarily do this with every Christian client. However, we do not believe that there is anything wrong with remaining curious of our clients' beliefs and also being knowledgeable of religious beliefs on relevant topics. If Joy would not have said, "The Bible," it's quite likely that I would not have said what I said. However, remaining curious is not synonymous with not knowing. If that were the case, of what use would therapy be?

We're aware that there are some postmodern therapists who believe that the best posture a therapist can take in therapy is a posture of not knowing, even asserting that their expertise as a therapist is in not knowing and that the expert in the therapy room is the client. Such an expert at being a nonexpert therapist would be similar to a mental health version of Sergeant Schultz, the character from the television show *Hogan's Heroes*.

We agree with Frank Thomas that it's useful for a therapist to be slow to know to help avoid jumping to conclusions. However, we get leery when some of our colleagues take this to the extreme whereby it's paradoxically clear that these therapists know that they don't know. Point this out to them, however, and they'll likely deny this to be true (we've seen this happen on numerous occasions). Herein lies another paradox. For their denial of this process-level reality due to their ignorance of the logical consequences of their own espoused beliefs, demonstrates that they, indeed, don't know! This exponentially paradoxical reality provides humor that is beyond humorous; for this is the type of humor that isn't intended nor attempted; it just is what it is.

Our postmodern colleagues will attempt to explain away this reality by invoking the assertion that postmodern theory is beyond logical thought. Again, they are correct, but only as a result of another paradoxical accident. Indeed, their thinking is beyond logic. Unfortunately, supporting this type of thinking necessitates praising illogic. For their own brand of thinking has led them into a trap they unknowingly set for themselves. C. S. Lewis ([1944] 1966) explained,

> A theory which explained everything else in the whole universe but which made it impossible to believe that our own thinking was valid, would be literally out of court. For that theory would itself have been reached by thinking, and if thinking is not valid that theory would, of course, be itself demolished. It would have destroyed its own credentials. It would be an argument which proved that no argument was sound—a proof that there are no such things as proofs—which is nonsense. (p. 24)

We'd also assert that most clients don't come to therapy seeking help from a therapist who is not knowing, especially if, similar to Ser-

IN THE OFFICE OF DR. SCHULTZ

geant Schultz, they really know what they claim not to know. We believe that clients enter the therapeutic process with exponentially more information about their life story than does their therapist. We also believe that clients don't expect their therapist to know everything about their life story at the outset of therapy. However, clients do seek help from someone who has some expertise and knowledge in the areas of providing help, guidance, and, at times, advice. If you don't believe us, just ask your clients, "How is it that I can be helpful?" After all, aren't they the experts?

As therapists, we ask the questions we do to gather information from our clients under the guise that with this information we can help our clients get to a better place. This is basic to our profession. If we have information that can be helpful to our clients based on their unique situation as they have espoused it, why in the world would we withhold this information from them? As therapists, we don't have to worry about rescuing God. God can take care of Himself. However, if we do not assist our clients with information that could be helpful to them in their life situation, just because this information is of a spiritual nature, what does that say about us? We believe that if we have information that can be helpful to a client in their unique life context, we are going to share that information. In our eyes, this makes us no different than the feminist therapist who suggests that a female client read a particular article or the family therapist who offers an article on parenting to a client whom the therapist believes could benefit from this information. Our position is, "Don't worry about rescuing God, for God can take care of Himself. However, be willing to assist clients when they are seeking our assistance."

8. Believe that being spiritually open-minded is the equivalent of being open to all spiritual beliefs.

In our research study, we included a measure to see if there was any relationship between the willingness of therapists to discuss spiritual issues in therapy and the way spirituality was talked about in therapy. We did this because we were pretty sure we were picking up on an interesting process in conversations we were having with some of our colleagues. In these discussions with other professionals about spiritual issues in therapy, there seemed to be a continuum of palatability with regard to the specific spiritual topics that were being addressed. The comfort levels of therapists seemed to be related to the way a client talked about spirituality and the words he or she used. For some, it seemed that talking about spirituality was no big deal. However, if this spirituality talk turned toward a personal God, their comfort level and willingness to engage in this type of conversation went down considerably. We thought we were seeing that spirituality talk was in vogue, just as long as God could be kept out of the equation. We'll even assert that some of our colleagues have experienced God phobia, an unhealthy fear of thinking and/or talking about God.

Based on this perceived process, we asked participants in our study some questions about their reported willingness to engage in certain types of spiritual conversations in therapy. We used a Likert-type scale to measure the participants' reported levels of willingness. We asked these therapists, "During a discussion with your client about his or her presenting problem, are you willing to talk about spirituality if the client introduces the topic?" We also asked them a very similar question, but changed one important word to see if there might be any difference in their responses. We asked them, "During a discussion with your client about his or her presenting problem, are you willing to talk about God if the client introduces the topic?" These results indicated that the therapists were significantly more willing to discuss spirituality than they were God in therapy, even if the client introduced the topic. This finding suggests that the difference in the meaning of these two words may be an important component in understanding therapists' willingness to integrate the spiritual realm and psychotherapy.

We believe that most therapists see spirituality as more inclusive and/or more palatable than they do God. However, it's important to note that this finding is not merely a revelation of therapeutic word games. This finding is not only statistically significant, but it's also clinically significant. Our questions were posed in a manner that would address the implicit integration of spirituality in therapy. So, these two questions, and the way they were posed, are predicated on the notion that these are the clients' own words. Therefore, this difference in therapists' willingness to discuss spiritual issues, if these issues are God related, may present potential problems for therapists and clients when working with clients who believe that their spiritual source is God. As previously discussed, Gallup polls (Gallup, 2001) indicate that approximately 95 percent of Americans believe in God.

Regardless of how people define God, we find it extremely interesting to note that therapists may not be as open-minded toward talking about God in therapy as they would be talking about spirituality in therapy. We don't personally believe that this is being open to the spiritual beliefs of the people, including 95 percent of Americans, who believe that God is their spiritual source.

On a side note, the term *religion* seems to have a process all its own. For many people in our field, religion appears to be a four-letter word. We can't count the times we've heard, "Religion? Don't get me started on religion. But I am a spiritual person." Interestingly, outside of therapy, we've found that a person's willingness to discuss religion does not necessarily increase in regard to a person's religiousness. In fact, we've never met colleagues who are more willing to give us their opinion about religion than are our atheistic and agnostic friends.

9. Practice God molding with your clients.

Let's put an artificial dichotomy on the table. We believe that most of the people in our society fall into two groups with regard to how they see themselves in regard to God and how they see God in regard to themselves. Many people believe in a God who "fits for me" or "works for me," and others believe in a God who wants to help them be molded to closer fit His image. Some people seek comfort from a God whom is molded in their image, others seek comfort from a God in whose image they believe they need to be molded. We've heard some professionals argue that every client molds God into his or her own image. Suffice it to say, this belief will undoubtedly lead to challenges for therapists who believe this when they're working with clients who do not agree with them. Abraham Lincoln (1866) confessed, "My great concern is not whether God is on our side. My great concern is to be on God's side" (p. 68).

Since we believe that this general dichotomy is true for society at large, we also believe that it's true inside the therapy room for both clients and therapists. A colleague once said, "When it comes down to it, we are just paid reframers." She said this partly in jest, so we offer it up partly in jest, but we also address her statement because there is some merit to what she's saying. A great deal of our work as therapists centers around helping our clients to see their life situations in new, unique ways that may offer them more freedom, flexibility, and/

or peace. As therapists and as human beings, we must acknowledge that our attempts to help clients in these endeavors will be influenced by what we believe can provide more freedom, flexibility, and/or peace. We must be aware of this process within the person of the therapist or else we'll likely take part in change processes where our values are very much at work, regardless of whether or not we're aware of this fact.

For example, as therapists who are also Christians, we must acknowledge that our own personal beliefs are also at work with regard to the concepts of freedom, flexibility, and peace. If we are to be honest with ourselves, we must acknowledge that we believe that greater freedom, flexibility, and peace can come from conforming ourselves to God's image, rather than conforming God to our image. If we don't acknowledge this, deny it, and/or ignore it, we run a greater chance of imposing these beliefs on our clients. Therefore, we'll own our beliefs. In his classic *Meditating on the Word,* Dietrich Bonhoeffer (1986) asserts:

> If it is I who say where God will be, I will always find there a God who in some way corresponds to me, is agreeable to me, fits in with my nature. But if it is God who says where he will be, then that will truly be a place which, at first, is not agreeable to me at all, which does not fit so well with me. . . . Not a place which is agreeable to us or makes sense to us a priori, but instead a place which is strange to us and contrary to our nature. Yet, the very place in which God has decided to meet us. (p. 45)

In owning our beliefs, we hope that other therapists will be willing to look at what they believe. So, we ask our colleagues to become more aware of their own biases that are systemically related to their own spiritual, religious, and/or life views. Although this may not seem like a difficult concept to understand and implement, we assert that there are subtle ways in which this lack of self-awareness influences the therapeutic process in some not so subtle ways. We believe the following real-life example will demonstrate this point quite well.

All-Inclusive Spiritual Group Therapy?

A couple of years ago, a friend and colleague told us a story about an interesting dynamic that she had observed as she supervised a therapeutic group. The group was titled "Women's Spirituality." It was advertised that this group was open to women who wanted to connect with the Divine, explore various spiritual paths, and share their thoughts on creating sacred space in life. Women of various spiritual perspectives took part in this group experience. In theory, the idea of having a place where women could get together and talk about their unique spiritual perspectives was an exciting and interesting idea. However, as we know, the reality is that well-intended theories don't always turn out as intended.

Before going into specifics, we think it might be helpful to briefly review the therapeutic factors in group therapy. The world's best-known group therapy practitioner and theoretician, Irvin Yalom (1985, pp. 3-4), divided the group therapeutic experience into the following eleven primarily significant factors:

1. Installation of hope
2. Universality
3. Imparting of information
4. Altruism
5. The corrective recapitulation of the primary family group
6. Development of socializing techniques
7. Imitative behavior
8. Interpersonal learning
9. Group cohesiveness
10. Catharsis
11. Existential factors

A number of various factors are at work in a group therapeutic setting. All of these factors can have a positive therapeutic effect on the lives of group members. However, these factors can potentially have a negative impact on group participants as well. Needless to say, it's important for group leaders to have a good understanding about the dynamics of group therapy so they can help create a safe environment for all participants with the hope that the therapeutic experience may also be helpful to the participants.

At one of the initial meetings of the women's spirituality group, one of the participants, Christy, spoke of an issue of uncertainty going on in her life. Christy reported that she was struggling with some issues and wasn't certain how she would handle them. She reported that part of her wanted to act in a certain way, but part of her didn't because this would be acting in a way that was contrary to her Christian beliefs. During the discussion that ensued, some of the other group members, likely out of a desire to help Christy, suggested that God wasn't necessarily against the actions that concerned Christy. Some group members explained that they believed in a God who was much different from Christy's God, and that their view of God had helped them experience freedom to be OK with what they did in similar situations. They went on to say that there's more than just one way to see God and that Christy would likely benefit if she were to become more open-minded and see God in a different way.

Indeed, just as Yalom suggested, the dynamics of attempting to instill hope, imparting of information, attempts at altruism, universality, interpersonal learning, and existential factors (just to name a few) were very much at work. Unfortunately, Christy never returned to the group. Later reports suggested that she had thought that others had not respected her Christian beliefs but were instead suggesting that everything would be better if she would adopt a more open-minded view of God as some of the others reportedly had done. Interestingly, she apparently experienced the very same thing that other people have told us turned them off to Christianity. In a nutshell, "You would be better off if you were to see God as we do."

This example is another challenge for those people who buy into the fallacious thinking involved in what we call, "the assumption of unidimensional proselytization." We've heard some in our field say, "Christianity is the only religion that teaches one to proselytize." However, research suggests that many within the walls of academia, and in society in general, would be wise to look at how they religiously proselytize in the name of open-mindedness. As G. K. Chesterton (1928) said, "These are the days when the Christian is expected to praise every creed except his own."

Again, we believe that Christy's group members and leaders had the best intentions in mind. We believe they were probably trying to help her experience freedom. However, what was going on outside of their cognitive box is what concerns us. For something completely different was going on inside of Christy's mind. This process-level reality likely led her to think, "They're trying to tell me how I should view God." Some may find God molding freeing. For Christy, this process was limiting, not freeing. This story led us to ponder the following question: When does a desire for all-inclusiveness become exclusionary?

Christy shared a dilemma. She didn't ask anyone to solve her dilemma, nor did she ask anyone to tell her how she should see God. She was a Christian and later reported that she was at peace with her faith. In this case, a desire for all-inclusiveness led Christy to feel, due to her spiritual beliefs, excluded. We're quite confident that no one wanted this to happen. The group participants and leaders were not bad people. In fact, we believe they had great intentions. The problem took place at a process level, because the people involved came from different spiritual paradigms, which impacted how they believed Christy needed to believe. This is a potential reality of God molding. This is a potential reality of deifying open-mindedness when it's carried out to its logical end. However, make no mistake, Christy, a spiritual woman attending a women's spirituality group, apparently didn't like the process of how her Christian beliefs about connecting with the Divine were approached.

10. Deify open-mindedness.

We believe that this is the single largest pink elephant that sits in the living room of our field today. Since we believe this is one of the main factors contributing to the learned avoidance, institutional aspiritualism, antireligious biases that lead to religious discrimination, and God phobia, that we see in our field today, we didn't believe we could do this issue justice without devoting an entire chapter to this topic. Therefore, as mice we move toward this elephant, cautious of its tusks, yet realizing that the elephant is scared of the truth. In the words of Martin Luther, "Truth is the most intolerable thing on Earth" (Luther, 1959, p. 1399). The truth is that this pink elephant is the Transformer du jour formerly known by the names value-free and value-neutral thinking.

Chapter 14

The Deification of Open-Mindedness

Their skepticism about values is on the surface: it is for use on other people's values: about the values current in their own set they are not nearly skeptical enough. And this phenomenon is very usual. A great many of those who "debunk" traditional or (as they would say) "sentimental" values have in the background values of their own which they believe to be immune from the debunking process.

C. S. Lewis
The Abolition of Man

It's very common to hear people use the term *open-minded* in our society today. In fact, the term is in vogue in a variety of settings. Whether a person hears a college student encouraging his or her friends to think open-mindedly or hears former President Bill Clinton suggesting the public should be open-minded about his use of executive privilege in defending his pardons (CNN, 2001b), it's quite common to hear calls for open-mindedness. We're not opposed to the concept of open-mindedness in and of itself. In fact, we would ask you to remain open-minded about our discussion of open-mindedness. A call for open-mindedness can indeed be helpful if it encourages people to thoroughly explore their own assumptions, beliefs, and/or biases. A call for open-mindedness can also be helpful if it encourages people to demonstrate love and respect toward fellow human beings. However, problems quickly arise when open-mindedness becomes the primary foundation upon which one builds one's major life views; in other words, when one deifies open-mindedness. We can't tell you how many times we've heard people say some derivation of, "The most important thing I can do as a human being is to stay open-minded."

As I (Peter) worked on the outline for this chapter, I overheard a conversation in a professional setting about the possibility of starting a spiritual growth group. Two colleagues were very excited as they discussed the possibility of starting such a group. Then I heard one therapist say to the other, "We'll have to do a group screening though, because we only want people who are open-minded." Needless to say, I wasn't surprised. Indeed, thinking open-mindedly about certain matters can be helpful. However, when a person deifies open-mindedness, this value leads to limitations that can be hurtful. We believe it's necessary to point out some of these limitations, because we've seen them become limitations within the therapeutic process, often because the therapist was blind to them.

Whether or not it is overtly acknowledged, when a person believes in open-minded thinking, he or she is also implicitly demonstrating an underlying belief in the existence of thinking that is not open-minded. We've heard a number of people in our profession talk about the traps of narrow-mindedness. We've also heard a number of people speak negatively about people whom they deem to be narrow-minded. Of course, people have the right to refer to other people as narrow-minded if they so choose. However, if they're doing this in the name of open-mindedness, they quickly run into trouble, regardless of whether or not they're aware of it. Consider the following question: *How is labeling someone as narrow-minded demonstrative of open-mindedness?*

It's impossible to be open-minded about everything. Some of you may suggest that this is self-evident. We wouldn't disagree with you. However, we would argue that the vast majority of the people who toss around the term open-minded more often than Sam Malone tossed out pickup lines on *Cheers* are not cognizant of the fact that they are being narrow-minded toward the beliefs of the people whom they are characterizing as narrow-minded. In other words, they are unaware of their own narrow-mindedness.

Although a person need not be a rocket scientist to grasp this concept, he or she does need to be open and honest with himself or herself about the simple limitations that exist within the realms of open-mindedness. Or else, the person will be controlled by the illusion that he or she can be completely open-minded, whereas "those narrow-minded people are not." Bert and Ernie address this type of logical reality on *Sesame Street* before children learn their multiplication tables. However, you would be amazed at the number of people within our field who have actually attempted to debate us on this point.

From our experiences with talking to people about this phenomenon, we've come to the conclusion that the deification of open-mindedness has often grown out of a desire to be loving, respectful, and welcoming of all people and to demonstrate a willingness to explore a person's own assumptions and beliefs. We couldn't praise these good intentions enough. In fact, we hope and pray that all individuals will learn to be more loving, caring, respectful, and welcoming of one another. Yet just as with many things in life, good intentions don't always lead to desired outcomes. Unfortunately, we saw this to be true in the case of Christy and her exclusionary all-inclusive group therapy experience.

Indeed, we should all aspire to be more loving and respectful of other individuals and groups. We don't believe that open-mindedness is the best pathway to achieve this desired goal, however, the people who try to live by the value of open-mindedness present themselves as being open-minded to all people, yet implicitly demonstrate that they are narrow-minded toward certain groups of people. We don't even believe this is a problem in and of itself. However, we do believe that the ignorance of this dynamic that is so often present in individuals who hold on to the "posture, position, or stance" of open-mindedness is a major problem. This dynamic demonstrates that many of the people who have deified open-mindedness are not even open to the dynamics in their own mind. Unfortunately, this lack of awareness can lead to vacant-mindedness.

Just as with so many other things in life, ignorance that goes unrecognized by the individual will likely become the ignorance that is recognized by the masses. If this mass enlightenment helps the individual to recognize his or her own ignorance, then good things can happen. However, if a person holds onto the deification of open-mindedness and claims that the ignorance lies within the others, then this ignorance will unfortunately lead the individual toward cognitive suicide.

VACANT-MINDED OPEN-MINDEDNESS

We were reminded of this a couple of years ago when a colleague took opposition to a point I (Peter) was making. This colleague claimed that he could truly be open-minded toward all people, because he didn't believe that his beliefs were any better than anyone else's beliefs, "period." I respectfully told him that I was certain that he believed that to be true, but that I was also certain that it was impossible to truly hold such a position. He disagreed with me saying, "You can't tell me what I believe."

I responded by saying, "In one sense I agree with you, I can't tell you what you believe. However, in another sense, I can demonstrate to you, based on your own espoused beliefs, that you don't even agree with yourself on this point."

He sarcastically laughed at me and then said, "Of course you'd think that, because unlike me you come from a position of believing that your beliefs are better than my beliefs."

"This may be difficult for you to hear, but you're right; I do believe that my beliefs are better than yours. I'll be open and honest with you about that. However, the interesting catch is that you believe that your beliefs are better than mine, too," I replied.

"That's not true. I don't believe that my beliefs are better than anybody else's beliefs."

"I've heard you say that before, but let's look at that in more depth. Let me ask you a question. If you don't believe your beliefs are better than anyone else's, why then do you hold the beliefs you hold?"

He responded, "I believe that my beliefs fit for me."

I said, "OK, what size shirt are you wearing?"

"What?"

"Just stick with me for a moment. What size is your shirt?"

"It's an XL."

I then asked him, "Why didn't you buy that same shirt in a small? Isn't it true that you bought that shirt because it fit you better than the small would have?"

"No, that's not the same thing," he said.

"Regardless, didn't you tell me that you didn't believe that your beliefs were any better than anyone else's beliefs?" I asked.

"OK, I believe what I believe because they work for me."

I then responded, "Can't you hear the parenthetical assertion implicitly leaping out of your last statement, 'I believe what I believe because my beliefs work *(better)* for me than do other beliefs'?"

He said, "No, Peter. You're wrong. That's not what I'm saying. You're putting words in my mouth. You're wrong. I don't believe that my beliefs are better than anyone else's beliefs."

I simply responded by saying, "Thank you for proving the validity of my point. For in telling me that I'm wrong, you're contradicting your own statement that you don't believe that your beliefs are any better than anyone else's beliefs."

We're not attacking the person who believes that he or she can be completely open-minded toward the beliefs of all people. In fact, we believe that most of these people have good intentions. We're simply pointing out that the problem is that their logic attacks itself. In the absence of uncertainty, indecision, or confusion, everyone believes what they believe because they believe these beliefs are better than the alternative beliefs. There is no inherent problem within this reality. To accept this is simply embracing reality rather than running from the truth. However, many people deny that they believe that their beliefs are better than other beliefs. Herein lies a big problem. As G. K. Chesterton (1900) said, "Impartiality is a pompous name for indifference, which is an elegant name for ignorance."

Some people have tried to explain away our assertion by suggesting, "Your motivation is simply to prove that others are wrong and you're right." However, the reality is that we simply desire to be consistent, true, noble, honorable, respectful, and pure. Since these are the things we strive for, the fact is that many times we find out that we're wrong. Yet in our opinion it's better to seek the truth when compared to the alternatives.

Some others have attempted to explain away our assertion by evoking the reality of preference. They've said that a person can prefer one thing and not think that it's better than the other things he or she doesn't prefer. To a certain degree, there's truth in this assertion. Indeed, we can prefer orange and call it our favorite color. In so doing, we need not take a negative view of red or blue or of the people who prefer red or blue to orange. However, by choosing orange as our favorite color, we've made a choice that fits us better than would red or blue. Again, this is not a problem. It makes sense to be open-minded to people whose favorite color is blue or red. However, we believe that there are some issues in life that take on a significance much greater than the "we're just talking about preference" argument can explain. It's this distinction, and make no mistake everyone makes some type of distinction, that presents problems for those who would suggest that preference can explain the larger issues of life.

Let's move this discussion about belief into the realms of spiritual beliefs. "Do you believe that Jesus of Nazareth was the Messiah and God in the flesh?" Hasn't the ante just been upped, or do you still believe that we're within the same preference paradigm as, "What's your favorite color?" For those who would suggest that we're still within the realms of preference, let's try another question. "Is it OK to sexually molest a child?" Is your answer to this question simply based on your own preference? If so, we'd suggest that you disengage from any further reading at this time and contact a qualified therapist in your area. If not, do you believe that your answer was based on your belief of what is right and what is wrong? If your response was based on your belief of what is right and wrong, what is the source of truth on which you base this belief?

It's been our experience that it's widely accepted in academia, and even in the fields of psychotherapy, to playfully question the belief that the Bible is God's inspired word. It's fine with us if people want to question Christians about their beliefs. In fact, as previously stated, we encourage people to question their own beliefs. Many of our colleagues have laughingly said things such as, "I can't believe that the people of the book actually believe that it contains the truths of life." This is also fine with us. In fact, we gladly entertain these types of conversations. However, if a person is going to go down that road with us, we simply ask him or her to be prepared to answer similar types of questions based on his or her belief perspectives.

I (Peter) was with a respected colleague one time when he made an offhand statement about people who believe in an absolute truth, followed by an assertion that all truth is subjective because all truth is socially constructed. I asked him if he rejected the idea of an overarching natural law or a divine being that is over all of humanity. He smiled, nodded his head, and said, "I believe that all truth is socially constructed." I responded, "If it's true that all truth is socially constructed, then on what basis can we ever judge whether what other societies construct to be true is right or wrong?" He smiled and invited me to tell him more. I said, "If all truth is socially constructed, then what right do we have to tell Hitler's Germany or cannibalistic societies that their socially constructed practices are not right?" He smiled, took a drink of his beverage, and changed the subject.

I have to admit that I can't claim authorship of the approach I used in that friendly discussion. It was borrowed from C. S. Lewis's classic, *The Poison of Subjectivism.*

> Out of this apparently innocent idea comes the disease that will certainly end our species (and, in my view, damn our souls) if it is not crushed; the fatal superstition that men can create values, that a community can choose its "ideology" as men choose their clothes. Everyone is indignant when he hears the Germans define justice as that which is to the interest of the Third Reich. But it is not always remembered that this indignation is perfectly groundless if we ourselves regard morality as a subjective sentiment to be altered at will. Unless there is some objective standard of good, over-arching Germans, Japanese and ourselves alike whether any of us obey it or not, then of course the Germans are as competent to create their ideology as we are to create ours. (Lewis, 1943, p. 224)

This quote was on my (PK) mind during a discussion I was having with some colleagues three days after the horrific terrorist attacks of September 11, 2001, on the World Trade Center and the Pentagon. We talked about how these attacks would likely lead many people to experience existential crises. During the course of this conversation, we also spent some time grieving and venting in healthy ways as we focused on our own self-care. Toward the end of our discussion, one of my colleagues commented, "I can't understand what would lead someone to commit such horrific acts." I took this opportunity to perhaps provide some insight into the thought processes of these terrorists. I said, "These terrorists probably believed that they were doing God's will when they committed those acts." Sensing an opportunity to lovingly challenge some of my colleagues with whom I had recently addressed their tendency to deify open-minded thinking, I then said, "Perhaps we should be more open-minded to their right to act on their beliefs and less judgmental." My good friends (by the way, some of whom now agree with me on this point) smirked as they caught the sarcasm that was saturating the example I had used to demonstrate the limitations of the "in all things, let us be open-minded" battle cry. However, one of my colleagues apparently thought I was serious and, while looking upward as if pondering what I had just said, responded by saying, "That's a good point. I haven't thought of it that way." I was amazed. Even I had not realized how pervasive and powerful a force open-mindedness had become in our society.

We can't count the number of times we've heard people make comments such as, "I've chosen to be open-minded. I'm not closed-minded like Christians are." We laugh at the biased illogic that is implicitly at work within this statement couched under the name of an all-loving open-mindedness. Some Christian thinkers have asserted that this type of thinking, whether consciously entered into or not, results in an attack on the spiritual beliefs of Christians. G. K. Chesterton (1906) asserted, "There are those who hate Christianity and call their hatred an all-embracing love for all religions."

We try to give people the benefit of the doubt. We believe that most people are simply unaware of the potential influence that deifying open-mindedness can have on other individuals. However, we've seen people who are very adept at using the phrase "you need to be more open-minded" as a covert trump card to manipulatively mandate another to agree with them or else risk being branded as narrow-minded. Make no mistake: the belief that those people who hold convictions about God and/or the Bible, just to name two, are narrow-minded doesn't demonstrate the existence of open-mindedness but rather demonstrates a person's own narrow-minded convictions that run counter to those convictions held by "those narrow-minded Christians."

Some will assert that being open-minded toward everyone else's beliefs is to attain a higher intellectual level. We couldn't disagree with them more. If being ignorant of a person's own biases and beliefs while pathologizing other people's beliefs, calling them narrow-minded, all under the name of open-mindedness, is reaching a higher intellectual level, then we suggest that our society has entered into an era where intellect has become equated with ignorance. Indeed, at times, ignorance can be bliss. However, we get a kick out of those who suggest that our opposition to deifying open-mindedness is simply a function of your own narrow-mindedness. As some say in the South, "That dog won't hunt."

We remind you of the story mentioned earlier of my (PK) colleague who stated that he believed in an omniscient God who didn't know everything. When I pointed out that he was suggesting that he believed in the concept of limited omniscience, he smiled and said that perhaps he did. When I asked him if he was aware of what the word *omniscience* meant, he said that he did. I then asked him, "Well, then, please tell me about this all-knowing God that you believe in who isn't all-knowing." Rather than answering my question, he suggested that since spirituality was a personal matter, he had the right to believe in whatever he wanted to and he didn't want to discuss it with me because he thought I might try to change his beliefs about God.

Recall that this was the same colleague who self-identified as a Christian even though he reported that he disagreed with many of Christ's teachings and did not believe that Jesus of Nazareth was truly the Messiah. Indeed, people can believe what they want. I wouldn't have tried to change his beliefs about God. However, my questions, based on his own logic, might have challenged him into seeing that illogic doesn't cease to be illogic simply because a person attaches God's name to the assertion. C. S. Lewis ([1944] 1996) unapologetically asserted:

> An open mind, in questions that are not ultimate, is useful. But an open mind about the ultimate foundations either of theoretical or of practical reason is idiocy. If a man's mind is open on these things, let his mouth at least be shut. (p. 59)

Are we the only ones who will *overtly* acknowledge that we embrace being closed-minded toward certain beliefs? If a person's beliefs border on idiocy, count us in the closed-minded group. If a person believes he or she has a right, due to his or her spiritual beliefs, to murder innocent Americans and Jews, brand us as closed-minded.

> Wherever there are Americans and Jews, they will be targeted. (Naseer Ahmed Mujahed, al-Qaida's chief military commander, in CNN, 2001a)

> We say our terror against America is blessed terror in order to put an end to suppression, in order for the United States to stop its support of Israel. . . . So we kill their innocents, and I say it is permissible in Islamic law and logic. (Osama bin Laden, in CNN, 2001a)

If a person believes that he or she can be completely open-minded and in the next breath talk about "those narrow-minded traditionalists," hey coach, sign us up for the closed-minded team. If a person reframes huge contradictions in his or her own philosophical thinking as "reaching a higher intellectual plain beyond logic," go ahead and brand us as two narrow-minded fools who can't be open-minded toward praising idiocy.

We'll own our narrow-mindedness! Will you own yours? If you don't, say hello to your role in the ongoing process of dumbing-down our society. This phenomenon has not escaped the notice of intelligent people in our society, regardless of their profession, such as comedian Dennis Miller.

> A chalk outline is slowly being drawn around common sense and most Americans can't even identify the victim. . . . Common sense has been defined as the quality of judgment necessary to know the simplest of truths. Well, nowadays simple truths are sighted about as often as Mary Hart on *Crossfire.* In the last twenty years we seem to have completely lost the ability to obey the natural laws around us. We no longer recognize things that are shockingly wrong anymore. We can't tell up from down, right from left, absolutely one hundred percent not guilty from double-murdering scumbag guilty. And we are getting stupider. (Miller, 1998, pp. 143-144)

QUESTIONS

- Have we reached the point in our society where a middle school student enrolled in the eighth grade can assert that he or she is a college student, and if we found out otherwise, we'd be guilty of being insensitive and narrow-minded toward his or her beliefs?
- Have we reached the point in our society where a student enrolled at Florida State University could, based solely on the fact that he or she is enrolled at FSU, call himself or herself a Longhorn and expect us, in the name of open-mindedness, to accept this as FSU's mascot?
- Have we reached the point in our society where we are so narrow-minded toward common sense that we must be open-minded to *every* belief or else be branded as insensitive narrow-minded jerks?

G. K. Chesterton ([1908] 1995) warned that

> The peril is that the human intellect is free to destroy itself. Just as one generation could prevent the very existence of the next generation, by all entering a monastery or jumping into the sea, so one set of thinkers can in some degree prevent further thinking by teaching the next generation that there is no validity in any human thought. (p. 38)

Indeed, open-mindedness is the reframed value-free, value-neutral, thinking du jour. In spite of the fact that many of our colleagues have grown to agree with us on this point, the strength of the defensiveness and the denial on the part of the open-minded believers should not be underestimated. We truly feel sorry for them. Many have failed to realize that open-mindedness, carried out to its logical conclusion, results in the demonstration of vacant-mindedness. Yet it has spread like wildfire throughout our society and relatively few seem to see that this pink elephant is laughing at us as it sits on our couch, influencing our children, eating our food, and expecting us to clean up the crumbs that it leaves behind. Synaptic transmission is occurring at a slower pace than Susan Lucci's exit from *All My Children*. Much of our society has been "group thought" into believing that we have progressed to a higher, more advanced, level of intellectual thinking. Many people have been tricked into believing in the absolute truth that there is no absolute truth.

In the same text, G. K. Chesterton ([1908] 1995) wrote,

> It is impossible without humility to enjoy anything—even pride. But what we suffer from today is humility in the wrong place. Modesty has moved from the organ of ambition. Modesty has settled upon the organ of conviction; where it was never meant to be. A man was meant to be doubtful about himself, but undoubting about the truth; this has been exactly reversed. Nowadays the part of a man that a man does assert is exactly the part he ought not to assert—himself. (pp. 36-37)

Many have been tricked into believing in the conviction that not having convictions (i.e., being ignorant of one's own convictions) is somehow demonstrative of being more loving and accepting. The concepts of right and wrong have gone out of fashion explicitly, but these concepts are still heavily relied upon, although selectively, as implicit trump cards. For you'll hear many people today say that it's insensitive (wrong) to speak of right and wrong, apparently ignorant of their own insensitivity. In the words of G. K. Chesterton and C. S. Lewis, respectively,

> Fallacies do not cease to be fallacies because they become fashions. (Chesterton, 1930)

> The uncritical acceptance of the intellectual climate common to our own age and the assumption that whatever has gone out of date is on that account discredited. You must find why it went out of date. Was it ever refuted (and if so by whom, where, and how conclusively) or did it merely die away as fashions do? If the latter, this tells us nothing about its truth or falsehood. (Lewis, 1955, pp. 207-208)

The question at hand is, "What do you personally intend to do?" Will you choose to accept the intellectual climate of our age, even if it means that you must stand "in praise of ignorance" as you actively ignore the pink elephant in the room? Will you choose to accept the intellectual climate of our age, even if it means that you must stand "in praise of idiocy" as you actively choose to clean up after the pink elephant? Regardless of your choice, ask yourself the following question: How then shall I think? In this matter, it may be prudent to consider the following words of G. K. Chesterton and Galileo, respectively,

> It is always easy to let the age have its head; the difficult thing is to keep one's own. (Chesterton, [1908] 1995, p. 107)

> I do not feel obliged to believe that the same God who has endowed us with sense, reason, and intellect has intended us to forgo their use. (Galileo)

Again, we believe that vacant-minded open-mindedness is more a result of unintentional ignorance than it is intentional aspiritualism. We believe that the open-minded movement originated with good intentions; love, respect, a slowness to judge, an openness to hearing others' opinions, and a questioning of a person's own beliefs. Indeed, these are good qualities to pursue. However, we don't believe that open-mindedness is the road that can best get us there.

> We have absolutely no difficulty regarding having to work in countries with many faiths, like India. We treat all people as children of God. They are our brothers and sisters. We show great respect to them. . . . Our work is to encourage these Christians and non-Christians to do works of love. (Mother Teresa, in Egan and Egan, 1989, p. 49)

We openly love and respect our Jewish, Muslim, Buddhist, etc., brothers and sisters cognizant of the fact that they believe that their spiritual beliefs work or fit better for them than do our Christian beliefs, and vice versa. In fact, in the spirit of love, we've had many respectful conversations with friends who self-identify with various spiritual traditions other than our own.

Let's always approach people with love and respect, without ignoring the fact that there are real clinical implications in not recognizing the intellectual implications of deifying open-mindedness. That's why we encourage everyone to explore their own beliefs about belief, life, truth, love, and spirituality so they can become more aware of their own beliefs and the influence that these beliefs can have on the therapeutic process.

Therapists have reported that clarity about their own personal sense of spirituality helped them feel more comfortable when talking with clients about their beliefs (Griffith and Griffith, 1997). Our research suggests that therapists who live out and/or truly practice their beliefs in life, regardless of whether they are religious or nonreligious persons, are more willing to discuss spiritual issues in therapy (Kahle, 1997). Based on these findings, it would seem sensible to hypothesize that therapists who are more at peace with their own beliefs may be more at peace with talking with others about their spiritual beliefs. This would suggest that a person's comfort level with having spiritual discussions in therapy may be more dependent on personal clarity and comfort with his or her own beliefs than pretending that he or she can be completely value-free and open-minded to everyone's beliefs. To ignore or to demonize conviction is, at best, to be ignorant of a person's own convictions. At worst, it is to actively engage in a campaign against the people with whom you disagree spiritually.

Let's be closed-minded toward supporting idiocy, pathologizing religious beliefs, demonizing groups of people, and aspiritualistic persecution. Let us acknowledge that we should all strive toward love, patience, kindness, humility, understanding, and intellectual health. According to Mother Teresa, "Our poverty should be true Gospel poverty, gentle, tender, glad, and openhearted, always ready to give an expression of love" (in Egan and Egan, 1989, p. 49).

Some may strive toward achieving all of these things in the name of open-mindedness. However, don't count us in. We will strive to grow in all these areas with the help of God and in the name of love. On this point, our minds are closed.

> *The object of opening the mind as of opening the mouth is to close it again on something solid.*
>
> G. K. Chesterton
> *Autobiography*

Chapter 15

God and Akelia: The Freedom That Binds

No matter what the world thinks about religious experience, the one who has it possesses a great treasure, a thing that has become for him a source of life, meaning, and beauty, and that has given a new splendor to the world and to mankind. . . . Where is the criterion by which you could say that such a life is not legitimate, that such an experience is not valid?

Carl Jung
Psychology and Religion

NURTURING THE CREATIVE GIFT WITHIN

There we were, the three of us, sitting in a room filled with so much tension you could have cut it with a knife. William was looking frustrated and sad, sitting in a chair with his head down respectfully listening to his mother. Chantel was scolding William for his failure to inform her that he was going to take the Texas Assessment of Academic Skills (TAAS) exam earlier in the day.

William had arrived at our office earlier than his mother on this particular day. They had taken different buses to get to our session. William had started to tell me about the written essay portion of this exam when Chantel walked into the therapy room. She smiled as she apologized for being slightly late to our session. After greeting him with a warm hug, she sat down in a chair next to her son. I (PK) encouraged William to continue telling me his story about the essay portion of the exam. As he talked, Chantel, with a confused look on her face, said, "What are you talking about, William? I thought you told me that the TAAS exam was next week?"

William responded, "I thought it was next week. I must have gotten my weeks mixed up."

Chantel quickly asked him, "What did you write your essay on?" William told her that he kind of talked about this and he kind of talked about that, not going into great detail about what he had written.

Based on his answer to his mother, it was very clear that William's gift of creativity had not flourished during the writing of his essay. Suddenly you could clearly see frustration come over Chantel's entire body. She interrupted William midsentence and said,

> You told me that the test was next week. You know that how well you do on that exam helps decide what level of class you'll get placed in next year. We were going to practice together on a story so you would be prepared to do well on that exam. I can't believe you got the weeks mixed up. William, this is another example of you not caring enough and not paying enough attention. Now, you're not going to get into the honors class we were hoping you'd get into. You just got yourself in trouble. What do you have to say for yourself?

William just sat there, slumped over, looking as if he could either yell out in frustration or start crying at any moment. But he sat there quietly, not saying anything in response to his mother's question. Chantel shook her head in frustration, took a big sigh, and looked away.

Not demonstrating the greatest therapeutic skill, I asked, "William, your mom asked you what you have to say for yourself." Total silence accompanied with no response at all. Finally realizing that I had become trapped in the content level, I immediately started to think about new process-level possibilities. I said,

> William, it looks like you're very frustrated. I think if I were in your shoes, I'd be frustrated, too. But, that's just a guess, because I don't know what it feels like to be in your shoes. But I think that both you and your mom are frustrated, and I want to help both of you. So let me ask you a couple of questions. Do you think you did as good a job on that essay as you would have liked?

William shook his head from side to side indicating "no." This was big progress. We had entered the realm of communication. I followed it up by asking, "What do you think got in the way of you being able to do your best?"

William sat there quietly for a few seconds before saying, "I guess I was lazy." Realizing that William had just given me an in to externalizing the problem, I said,

> You know, you've always impressed me as a creative young guy. I've even heard your mom talk about what a creative storyteller you are. Could you take a deep breath and maybe tell us a story about how laziness got the best of you?

Still looking down, he nodded his head yes. His mother had turned her attention back toward her son just in time to see him nod his head. Then, after some time to gather his thoughts, William took a deep breath and said, "Once upon a time, in a planet far, far away, there was an alien named Lazo. Now one day, Lazo thought, 'I'm going to go visit a boy named William . . .'"

Rather than continue to tell the story of this session from my memory, we thought it would make more of an impact to let you see what William and Chantel brought with them to our session the following week. It's an excellent summary of what we discussed in this session. But, more important, what they brought in was the result of mother and son collaboratively working together, to creatively integrate his strengths of creativity and writing with their faith, to fight against "Lazo" (i.e., laziness). The following is a copy of the story written by Chantel and William. (Spelling errors have been retained.) Figure 15.1 is the cover graphic that the clients designed to go with the story.

> This is the story of Akliea and "D" Destructo, they are opposite forces who can influence one's actions and decisions. Akelia is one who protects and his forcefield beams joy, love, obedience, truth, discipline, and faith. "D" Destructo is one who destroys and his forcefield beams anger, disobedience, hatred, lying, mischief, and trouble.
>
> "D" Destructo is also known as the thief that comes to steal, kill, and destroy, but Akelia is the one who gives abundant life to all who surrender to his will. (John 10:10) "D" Destructo is very

crafty he is a *transformer* who can change his image. For example, on February 25, 1997 he transformed into Lazio a lazy force that tempted me while I was taking my TAAS reading and writing test.

Lazo came right up from the pits of the earth, he tapped me on the right shoulder I looked to the right and no one was there then he tapped me on my left shoulder and to my surprise no one was there. He spoke to me in a lazy voice "this is enough William, don't put any more on the paper." Akelia immediately spoke in a strong firm voice "ignore him William you know that "a person who doesn't work hard is just like a person who destroys things." (Prov 18:9)

Lazo declared war! He told me that it was okay to be a little lazy and I thought to myself he's right everyone is lazy every once in awhile. I really didn't feel like working after all I had just finished reading multiple choice paragraphs and I was tired, but the first words that came out of Akelia's mouth was "you can do all things through Christ William who strengthen you. (Philip 4:13) Lazo replied, "why do you need Christ to strengthen you when all you have to do is just enough to get away" and that is exactly what I done. I done just enough to get by and guess what Lazo won, I gave him the power to win when I became disobedient and lazy. I should have listened! I should have listened to Akelia when I had the chance! I guess you can say I learned my lesson this time and I will beware of Lazo and remember to never do enough just to get by when I can do my best!

We trust you'll agree with us that there is something special about reading the exact words these clients chose to use to tell their unique story. William would later explain in a transition session when John was taking over as the primary therapist (due to the end of my practicum training) that Akelia, the protector, was a guardian who watched over you and helped you out in life. He said, "My mom is an Akelia, you (John) are an Akelia, Peter's an Akelia, but God is the ultimate Akelia." William reported that he had first heard of Akelia in the Scouts. Even though he was initially concerned that I would think he was crazy for telling this story, William found a creative way to help him fight against the influence of laziness.

"D" DESTRUCTO VS AKELIA

FIGURE 15.1. Cover graphic that accompanied William and Chantel's story.

TRACKING THE INFLUENCE OF SUCCESS

A couple of weeks later, William and Chantel showed up to a session carrying "Chapter Two" based on some struggles he had experienced during this week. Rather than telling you what issue he was challenged with that week, we'll let you read the chapter of his own words. We trust you'll be able to figure it out.

> Have you ever been attack by *DISRESPECTO?* If you have, than you will be able to understand this segament of this story. A couple of weeks ago I had a battle with him and I lost. The reason why I lost is because I disrespected my mother and she was very upset! I know that disrespect is not a part of God after all Exdous 20:12 says "Honour thy father and thy mother : so that your days upon the earth may be long."
>
> That day I knew I gave my mother a reason to discipline me and I knew that the bible says, "Do unto to others as you would have them do unto to you so I should not have disrespected be-

> cause I don't like to be disrespected. I have worked hard this week be respectful.
>
> I have not disrespected my mother, teachers or peers this week. I done what my mother asked me to do, I have not rolled my eyes at her and when I got angry I did not disrespect anybody.
>
> I had a good week at school I did not disrespect my teachers I M.Y.O.B. and done all of my work and made good grades on all of my tests. I respected my peers in a way that I wanted to be respected.

Weeks later during that transition session we briefly mentioned, Chantel commented that she was very pleased with her son because she had seen great improvement in his self-control, which she partially attributed to his increased awareness of his issues. The following is a brief excerpt from the transcript of that session.

PETER: What you have seen William use to help him increase his self-control and increase his awareness? What are the things you attribute his success to?

CHANTEL: One thing I know is that this counseling has been a big help. The things that we learned in here, such as having William get to the point where he thinks and is more aware before he acts out. Plus praying and studying the Bible and just being there, just being there for William, because one point in time, like last night, he told me about what the children used to do to him on the bus . . . and he said, "And when I told you how they treated me you act like you didn't care and I would go to bed and I would cry because you acted like you didn't care." And I was like, "William, it wasn't that I didn't care, I was just trying to let you see that it really didn't matter what they say." I don't know . . . it was just reading and studying and we did this scripture last night and what was that . . . "A soft answer turns away wrath, but grievous words stirs it up" . . . and I said, "William, do you know what that means?" I had to say it over for him again and he said, "Oh yeah, I know what that means." And I said, "See you don't always have to speak out or lash out or you can say it in a smoother way and don't keep it going" or something like that. At one point I had William looking up scriptures on anger and he even had to carry them to school with him to read them when things got bad for him.

INTERNALIZING PERSONAL AGENCY FOR HEALTHY CHANGE

Indeed, by externalizing the problem and respecting his faith, William stopped being the problem, the problem became the problem, and mother and son were able to rally together, with the help of God and Akelia, to successfully fight against Lazo and Disrespecto. This freedom helped William creatively access his faith as a source of strength helping him to see positive, concrete changes, both at school and at home. During our work with William and his mother, William returned to his regular school, and his mother and teachers reported that his behavior and academic work improved dramatically. Whoever thinks that the spiritual faith of a client can't be respected and encouraged in such a way as to help clients achieve concrete goals in therapy never met Chantel, William, or Akelia.

Perhaps those who still think that spiritual faith can't lead to powerful, concrete change might benefit from some therapeutic work to help them fight against the influence of "Blindspoto" and "Godphobio." Regardless, to help us end this chapter we're going to embrace our too-often-ignored friend "Redundancyo."

> *No matter what the world thinks about religious experience, the one who has it possesses a great treasure, a thing that has become for him a source of life, meaning, and beauty, and that has given a new splendor to the world and to mankind. . . . Where is the criterion by which you could say that such a life is not legitimate, that such an experience is not valid?*
>
> Carl Jung
> *Psychology and Religion*

Chapter 16

In Reverence of Power: Moving Toward Competence

Not that we are competent in ourselves to claim anything for ourselves, but our competence comes from God.

The Apostle Paul
(II Corinthians 3:5, NIV)

WHAT IS POWER?

Of course, not all clients are similar to William and Chantel. Indeed, those two have a special gift. However, the power of spirituality in therapy is not relegated to the example of William and Chantel. The power of spirituality in therapy has also been experienced by the Edwards, the Carolines, the Ryans, the Lisas, the Shannons, and the Joys of the world. *The fact is that many clients have had positive therapeutic experiences and have made healthy changes in their lives, in part, due to their therapists' willingness to approach therapy in reverence of power.* Sure, integrating spirituality and therapy does not guarantee that positive, healthy changes will always occur. It isn't a sure thing. However, what is?

We get a kick out of professionals who work hard at critiquing theories and interventions to prove that they are limited and therefore cannot ensure therapeutic success. Friends, don't bother wasting your time. We'll own it. Our submarine has been turned around and we are heading full speed ahead embracing the idea that spiritual conversations will not always lead to the desired change clients are seeking. However, we take comfort in knowing that there are no sure things when it comes to therapeutic approaches and/or interventions. However, one item that is a sure thing in therapy is that if you practice for any length of time at all, you'll be confronted with God talk in therapy. Therefore, the more operative question would appear to be, "What can I do, to the best of my abilities, to strive toward therapeutic competence when spiritual and/or religious issues arise in therapy?"

The following are ten more therapeutic principles therapists can embrace to help them move toward therapeutic competence when integrating spirituality and psychotherapy. In no way do we want to give you the impression that we believe that you'll automatically become a spiritually competent therapist by simply following these ten principles. It would be nice if it were that easy. We believe, however, that it takes a great deal of work, motivation, and training to become an effective therapist in integrating spirituality and therapy. In fact, some have argued that it might even be wise to move toward a recognized area of expertise designed for those therapists who would like to specialize in the integration of spirituality and therapy. We're not opposed to that idea. Indeed, it's very difficult, at times, to work with spirituality in therapy. However, we don't want to fall into the possible trap of passively supporting passive avoidance, active avoidance, passive proselytization, and active proselytization due to the possibility that this may, one day, reach such a status in our field. It may, or it may not. Regardless, in the mean time, there are clients all over the world who are today introducing spirituality into therapeutic conversations with therapists who have not had any training in this area. We believe that now is the time to actively face the pink elephants in our field to help start the work toward spiritually competent therapy. We hope that the process and the end goal are not seen as mutually exclusive.

> *Peace is not merely a distant goal that we seek, but it is a means by which we arrive at that goal.*
>
> Martin Luther King Jr.

TEN WAYS THERAPISTS CAN WORK TOWARD SPIRITUALLY COMPETENT THERAPY

1. Understand that spirituality and religion are powerful and important concepts for most of our clients.

- Ninety-five percent of Americans surveyed believe in God (Gallup, 2001).
- Ninety-two percent of Americans surveyed identify with a religious group (Gallup, 2001).
- At least 90 percent of Americans surveyed desire some type of religious education for their children (Hoge, 1996).
- Eighty-six percent of Americans surveyed reported that religion is very or fairly important in their lives (Gallup News Service, 2002).
- Seventy-five percent of Americans surveyed reported they pray on a daily basis (Gallup, 1999).
- Approximately 76 percent of Americans surveyed believe the Bible is the actual or inspired word of God (Gallup News Service, 2001).
- Sixty-six percent of Americans surveyed reported they would prefer a counselor who is religious (Gallup Poll Monthly, 1993).
- Many therapists report that clients encourage them to talk about God in therapy (Kahle, 1997).
- Many of our clients have reported they have made gains with spiritually inclusive therapy that they never made with more traditional therapeutic approaches.

2. Understand that spirituality is *not* a therapeutic technique or a fad.

Some time back in a brochure for a professional conference, we saw a presentation on integrating spirituality in therapy titled, "Spirituality: A Technique for Family Therapy." That title caught our eye. With our sincere apologies to the presenters, we openly admit that we didn't attend that workshop. It could have been an excellent workshop. Our comments are not directed toward the presenters, for we've seen titles similar to this one used in many other presentations and articles over the past eight years. Our point is best made with the question, Is spirituality a therapeutic technique? We think not. Although we're encouraged that spirituality has received increased attention at conferences and in journals in recent years, we're concerned that spirituality risks becoming a fad of the field, losing popularity, eventually joining the mothball ranks along with trephination, bleeding, free association, biofeedback, and the empty chair.

In thinking about this, I (John) was reminded of an analogous process that I've witnessed on a number of occasions in the most interesting place, a youth soccer match. When I watched my nephews and niece play soccer in their first year, I was amazed at how many little children can bunch up together around such a small object. If you've never attended a youth soccer game, whenever and wherever the ball is kicked, all the little kids chase after the ball. Rather than the players being spread out across the field based on their positions, as would be seen in a more advanced soccer match, it's as if the ball has a magnetic pull on each and every child bringing them together en masse. Meanwhile, in a cute display of naive innocence, none of the little children appear to have a clue, nor a care, that they are involved in a process that is, let us just say, not the most functional way to achieve balanced success.

It seems that our field has the tendency of thinking that we've found something new, talking about it for some time period, and then jumping on the next bandwagon that comes along. This type of temporal narcissism, the assumption that whatever is newer is therefore better, concerns us. Unfortunately, this reality has not gone unnoticed by people in our society. According to Dennis Miller (1998), "You know, I would put more faith in psychotherapy if it weren't so susceptible to every goofy trend that rolls down the Mental Health Freeway" (p. 123). We encourage all of us toward humility. Spirituality is not some type of technique that a therapist can manipulate to achieve a desired outcome. We all need to understand that, as therapists, we are not the most powerful aspects of people's lives. We need not think that we're the ultimate power to help empower our clients. In reality, we are actually more likely to get in the way of the process if we, either intentionally or unintentionally, believe we're more important than we are.

Bagger Vance, the character played by Will Smith in the hit film *The Legend of Bagger Vance* (2000), speaking as a golf caddie and spiritual advisor, offers advice that therapists would be wise to heed and apply in their work with clients. Speaking to Rannulph Junuh (played by Matt Damon) as they watch Bobby Jones approach a shot, Bagger says,

> He's practice swinging, almost like he's searching for something. Then he finds it. Watch how he's settling himself right

> into the middle of it. Feel that focus. He's got a lot of shots he could choose from, duffs and tops and skulls. But there's only one shot that's in perfect harmony with the feel. . . . There's a perfect shot out there trying to find each and every one of us. All we got to do is get ourselves out of its way. . . . I can't take you there (Junuh), just hopes I can help you find a way.

If it weren't so alarming, we'd be amused at some therapists who ask, "Should God and/or spirituality be allowed in therapy?" What a narcissistic position to assume that therapists have the professional right to exclude from therapeutic conversations something that is so powerfully important to so many clients. According to C. S. Lewis ([1947] 1996), "What we call man's power is, in reality, a power possessed by some men which they may, or may not, allow other men to profit by" (p. 66). When it comes to the realm of integrating spirituality in therapy, we would ask, Can we help empower clients without understanding that we are disempowered?

3. Understand that it's OK to be humbled as a therapist.

Spiritual conversations will not always, in and of themselves, help clients gain the type of change they are seeking. The good news is that no therapeutic approach, in and of itself, will always help clients achieve their goals. Embrace this reality, and you'll take an important step toward embracing humility.

My (PK) clinical mentor, Delane Kinney, taught me a very important lesson several years ago as she was leading a workshop on narrative therapy. One of the audience members asked one of those questions that wasn't really a question. This workshop attendee, perhaps somewhat threatened by narrative ideas, asked Delane, "Yes, but what about in the cases when narrative therapy doesn't work? What do you have to say about that?" Delane, in a very calm and graceful manner, responded,

> In that regard, I would simply suggest that narrative therapy is no different than any other approach to therapy. In my opinion, every good therapist who has practiced for some time understands that he or she will make mistakes in therapy and understands that no therapeutic approach guarantees therapeutic success.

Although I'm certain Delane didn't conceptualize this experience in this manner, she taught me a great deal about the importance of turning one's submarine around and embracing the potential limitations and dangers of life, inside and outside of the therapy room.

I (PK) was recently reminded of how helpful it can be to be humbled as a therapist. I was working with a woman, Joanne, who was going through a divorce process. During our first session, Joanne quoted scripture about six times, integrating these words into her therapeutic story as she told me about the sadness and disappointment she was experiencing. At the end of the session, Joanne commented, "But I'm trying to keep a positive focus because I know I'll get through this." Sensing an opportunity to affirm her perspective I said, "You sound like you're taking an excellent approach toward the grieving process. It will take some time, but I, too, am confident that you'll feel better in the future because it says in scripture that all things will work together for good" [based on Romans 8:28]. Joanne responded, "I'd like to come back and talk with you some more, but I need to tell you that I got a weird feeling when you said that. It reminded me of my grandfather. He was a minister and he used to verbally abuse me." I thanked her for sharing that information with me and I apologized for assuming that it would be OK to integrate scripture into our work. She smiled and thanked me for my apology.

This is an excellent example that demonstrates the importance of guarding against the assumption of knowing and that, even if we make a mistake in therapy, it doesn't necessarily mean that the therapeutic relationship will be damaged beyond repair. In fact, some weeks later, Joanne told me that she'd like to integrate her spirituality and her belief in scripture into our work. I said I'd be happy to, but told her that I was somewhat hesitant due to our previous experience, so I'd need her help in teaching me how she'd like it integrated. She smiled and said, "You're fine. I trust you now, but I'll let you know if it feels weird again."

Months later, Joanne was doing great, after experiencing a number of ups and downs as she went through a process of grieving her divorce and the loss of her previous dreams. I asked her, "Joanne, what's helped you get to the point where you are today?"

She said, "I feel so much better because my relationship with God has improved immensely. I know that He's going to take care of me no matter what."

I smiled and responded, "So believing that God is going to take care of you has helped you feel better?"

"No! I didn't say *believing,* I said that I *know* that God is going to take care of me!"

"I'm sorry I used the wrong word. Indeed, there is a big difference between believing something versus knowing something, isn't there?"

Joanne smiled and said, "You better believe it."

4. Understand that spiritual differences are important.

It's important for therapists to honor the fact that there are spiritual differences with neither minimizing nor marginalizing these differences. There are reasons for the existence of many different religions. There are reasons for the existence of many different denominations within the same religion. We would encourage the people who have great intentions in pushing for all-inclusiveness to become aware that their push can, at times, become exclusionary. It is OK to have separate umbrellas. When we're talking about two vastly different spiritual approaches, we're often talking about two different paradigms. Oftentimes, it would be best if people didn't attempt to achieve the impossible by shoving them into the same paradigm. For example, when you're talking about pantheism, monotheism, and atheism, realize that you're talking about different "isms." People have the right to believe what they want to believe. The monotheist who attempts to inform the pantheist or atheist that his or her beliefs are misguided is susceptible to the same type of frustration that the pantheist or atheist is if he or she attempts to inform the monotheist that he or she finds the monotheist's beliefs "limiting because you only believe in one God." For this is the very nature of their belief system. Oftentimes, they are even aware that the other sees their paradigm as limiting. Indeed, that is why they hold different beliefs. Thomas Paine ([1794] 2001) openly confessed, "I believe in one God and no more; and I hope for happiness beyond this life" (p. 319).

We often wonder why some in our society seem to have lost the ability to respectfully disagree with each other. Disagreement, in and of itself, is not a bad thing. Yet so many people in our society seem to have a problem with "people who can't agree with me," and are simultaneously ignorant of the fact that they, too, are disagreeing with those people. Unfortunately, this process often leads to the members of one group referring to the members of the other group, in some way, shape, or form, as either malcontents or narrow-minded traditionalists. This results in problems at a process level due to disagreement at the content level; hence problems at both levels. Try to lovingly and respectfully agree to disagree. At times, even this can be fun.

One of my (Peter) dearest friends in the field is someone who self-identifies differently than do I in the areas of gender, race, ethnicity, sexual orientation, spirituality, and political affiliation. Yet because we have a foundation of love and mutual respect, our relationship has grown to be very strong largely due to the love and respect we have for each other as human beings. Because of this, we have the ability to have discussions in which we lovingly and respectfully disagree with each other. She once told me, "One of the main problems I have with Christianity is that it's based on the belief that there is only one way to get to heaven. In a sense, there is only one right way to believe. I believe there is more than one right way to believe." I lovingly responded, "So, based on what you said, would you say that you believe that the right way to believe is to believe that there is not one right way to believe?" We both smiled and laughed together. It's OK to disagree. It's OK to recognize that we are often talking about different umbrellas from under different umbrellas. It's OK to know that your colleagues think your beliefs are out there. It's OK to do all these things, but let us all do them lovingly with gentleness and respect.

5. Understand that effective therapeutic work lies along a continuum between the end points of avoidance and proselytizing.

The Dr. Godcrutches and Dr. Myways of the therapeutic world are often left wondering why more clients don't return for a second session.

6. Understand that there are many potential traps a person can fall into if he or she believes in God. (The following is not an exhaustive list.)

- Positioning himself or herself as "spiritually one-up"
- Attempts to rescue God
- Claims of divine knowledge (i.e., speaking as if you are God rather than about God)

- Proselytizing
- Debating doctrine and/or beliefs
- Mandating specific beliefs
- The entrapment of knowing

7. Understand that there are many potential traps a person can fall into if he or she deifies open-mindedness. (The following is not an exhaustive list.)

- Unrecognized God phobia
- Unrecognized aspiritualism
- Both active and passive support of institutional aspiritualism
- The practice of God molding
- The faith, but only in moderation blind spot
- The assumption of a narrow-minded-free open-mindedness
- The entrapment of exclusionary all-inclusiveness
- The assumption of unidimensional proselytization
- The assumption of unidirectional conversion therapy
- The entrapment of knowing
- The entrapment of not owning

8-10. Understand the individual and systemic dynamics of the three main powers, the therapeutic triangle of power, present in psychospiritual therapy.

- The power of God
- The power of the client
- The power of the therapist

> *You would have no power over me if it were not given to you from above.*
>
> Jesus to Pilate, John 19:11

Since we're presenting this from our belief system, we chose authenticity over political correctness. However, for those of you who find God offensive or limiting and/or continue to experience God phobia, please feel free to put this first dimension into your own words. The important thing for us as therapists is to explore our own beliefs about the various dimensions of power in the therapeutic relationship.

The therapist has the power to believe in whatever he or she wants to believe. The therapist has the power to be aware of his or her beliefs, to be ignorant of his or her beliefs, and even to deny that he or she has beliefs. The therapist has the power to be aware of the fact that his or her beliefs will influence his or her work as a therapist.

The therapist has the power to respect his or her client's beliefs. The therapist has the power to respect his or her client's desire to either talk or not to talk about God and/or spirituality in therapy. The therapist has the power to constrain conversations about God and/or spirituality in therapy. The therapist has the power to ignore a client's desire to include God and/or spirituality in therapy. The therapist has the power to mandate that there be conversations about God and/or spirituality in therapy.

The therapist has the power to believe in a God who is powerful. The therapist has the power to not believe in a God who is powerful. The therapist has the power to believe in thirteen and one half gods who are powerful. The therapist has the power to believe that he or she is the most powerful and important source of help in his or her clients' lives. According to Erich Fromm ([1941] 2001), "The lust for power is not rooted in strength, but in weakness" (p. 51). The therapist has the power to believe that God is an illusion and/or an infantile form of wish fulfillment. The therapist has the power to use cocaine and smoke over twenty cigars per . . . sorry about that. We got off track a little bit. Anyway, power is a multidimensional force that is profoundly important to be aware of in the life of psychotherapy. We would encourage every therapist to join us and stand in reverence of power. Dennis Miller (1996) humorously observed,

> So those are the kinds of power. The only other thing you need know is that we all crave power. Whether it's heading a major entertainment company or just spraying that cockroach in your kitchen with a steady stream of Raid and pretending you're Red Adair on a blazing oil platform in the middle of the Caspian Sea. Face it, we all get off on power. (p. 65)

REVISITING SELF-REFLEXIVITY

Since we've been encouraging you throughout this book to explore your own beliefs in open, honest, and ethically responsible ways, we need to practice what we preach, so to speak. We need to let you know that we used deception earlier in the book. Thus, it's our ethical responsibility to inform you of our use of deception and to ensure that you're sufficiently debriefed with regard to why deception was used.

In Chapter 1, we invited you to take part in a self-reflexive exercise where we used a quotation to help you explore your own biases, assumptions, and beliefs associated with working with a client who may have made this particular statement: "Jesus is eternally right. History is replete with the bleached bones of nations that refused to listen to him. May we in the twentieth century hear and follow his words—before it is too late."

Our intent was to have you explore your own cognitive and emotional reactions that resulted from imagining what it would be like for you personally to work with a client who would hold such beliefs. We asked you to consider whether it would be easy or difficult for you to work with an individual who would make such a statement. We also asked you whether or not you would characterize a person who would make such a statement as narrow-minded or open-minded. Through this self-reflexive exercise, we also asked you to consider whether or not you agreed with the statement. We then attributed the statement to a famous individual, Jerry Falwell, and asked you similar questions to help you explore whether anything had changed for you once we attributed this statement to Jerry Falwell. However, we need to let you know that Falwell is not the author of this statement. Another famous American who was also a Baptist minister is the true author of this statement: "Jesus is eternally right. History is replete with the bleached bones of nations that refused to listen to him. May we in the twentieth century hear and follow his words—before it is too late" (Dr. Martin Luther King Jr., [1963] 1981, p. 57).

Did anything just change within you? If so, why? If not, why? Is it easier or more difficult for you to imagine working with King as a client than it would be to work with Falwell? If so, why? If not, why? Do you think that the person who made this statement was a narrow-minded Christian? If so, why? If not, why?

We've done similar exercises at conferences over the years and have received some interesting feedback from colleagues across the nation. Most of our colleagues have told us that they loved the exercise, not in spite of, but because they were humbled. One therapist, who attended one of our workshops in 2002, sent me a note to thank me for the experience. This colleague wrote,

> Dr. Kahle, I wanted to let you know how much I enjoyed your presentation. . . . My eyes were opened to the fact that I really needed to reflect on my assumptions and beliefs about religion. . . . I gained so much from your presentation. Thanks so much.

Some other therapists have demonstrated that they have some more self-reflexive work to do. One colleague commented, "I guess I never realized that he [King] was narrow-minded like that." Another colleague suggested at the conclusion of our workshop, "This exercise doesn't really demonstrate anything. Our reaction is contextually dependent on our knowledge of these two men." John responded in a very calm, kind, and insightful manner by saying,

> Sir, we would agree with you that your reaction to this exercise is context dependent. We would simply encourage you to consider that the context on which your reaction depended was an internal context. Indeed, this context is uniquely different for each and every therapist.

Several years ago, we went through separate processes of discovering that our beliefs about open-mindedness, right and wrong, truth, justice, liberty, freedom, and other value-free values that were addressed in our training had limited us from being able to *truly* respect everyone with whom we worked in therapy. This was not easy to admit, but we had to be brutally honest with ourselves. We both thought that we had a great deal of understanding because we were knowledgeable about the newest theories and the latest research in our field. We considered ourselves to be more postmodern than our postmodern colleagues, deconstructing absolute truth, absolute moral laws, and even Christian counseling. We didn't know at that time that someone whom we respected from a distance would later teach us a great deal about our own narrow-mindedness and temporal narcissism. We came to realize that a person cannot experience true freedom in the future unless he or she also experiences true freedom toward the past. Through our own temporal narcissism we had unintentionally participated in a discriminatory process that is still very alive today. C. S.

Lewis called this pink elephant we call temporal narcissism "chronological snobbery," and Martin Luther King Jr. referred to it as "the cult of inevitable progress." Others have also noticed this phenomenon, including G. K. Chesterton ([1908] 1995).

> Tradition means giving votes to the most obscure of all classes, our ancestors. It is the democracy of the dead. Tradition refuses to submit to the small and arrogant oligarchy of those who merely happen to be walking about. (p. 53)

Through reading what some might label an old book, we were reminded that reading about a person is a very different experience than reading the actual works of a person. Indeed, King taught us a great deal about love, respect, freedom, intellect, faith, and both/and thinking, while espousing beliefs that many people of today (yes, even some therapists) would pathologize and label as narrow-minded words that demonstrate an underlying hatred for people who disagree with him. In his classic, *Strength to Love* (1963), we found a gift to the therapeutic community that provides a great deal of insight into his spiritual beliefs. In this work, King taught us more about self-reflexivity than we could ever hope to teach anyone. How did he do this? He simply spoke from his heart about his spiritual beliefs and convictions. In so doing, he taught us both a great deal about ourselves as persons of the therapist.

The key to integrating spirituality and psychotherapy is to understand that we must be aware of our internal context to help our clients with their internal context. In a sense, we must "know thyself," if we are to help our clients know themselves. We must be able to know how we see things and learn how our clients see things. We must know what we believe, so we aren't threatened by what our clients believe. We must own our beliefs or else our beliefs will own us, and likely the therapeutic process. We must stand in reverence of power, knowing that we are only a part of the equation. We must learn to sit with similarity without assuming we are the same. We must learn to sit with difference without assuming we are completely different. This is embracing the reality of therapy, rather than being controlled by this reality. This is the way toward a deeper appreciation of the power of spirituality in therapy.

> We cannot give what we do not have. That is why it is necessary to grow in love. And how do we grow in love? By loving, loving until it hurts. You and I must examine ourselves. Our presence, our voice, what does it give to the people? (Mother Teresa, in Egan and Egan, 1989, p. 119)

THE EXAMINATION CONTINUES

How do you define liberty?

> Then I saw all the brown birds were trying to kill the yellow one, and that started my thoughts off as it might anybody's. Is it always kind to set a bird at liberty? What exactly is liberty? First and foremost, surely, it is the power of a thing to be itself. In some ways the yellow bird was free in its cage. It was free to be alone. It was free to sing. In the forest, its feathers would be torn to pieces and its voice choked forever. Then I began to think that being oneself, which is liberty, is itself limitation. We are limited by our brains and our bodies; and if we break out, we cease to be ourselves and perhaps, to be anything. (Chesterton, 1929, p. 259)

How do you define freedom?

> Freedom to me is not going out and doing what you want to do. Anyone can do that, and lots of people are doing it. Freedom is "To have the power to do what you know you ought to do." Most people know what they ought to do, but they don't have the power to do it. They're in bondage. (McDowell, 1977, pp. 117-118)

Do you believe in right and wrong?

> Moral principles have lost their distinctiveness. For modern man, absolute right and absolute wrong are a matter of what the majority is doing. Right and wrong are relative to likes and dislikes and the customs of a particular community. We have unconsciously applied Einstein's theory of relativity, which properly described the physical universe, to the moral and ethical

> realm . . . mentality has brought a tragic breakdown of moral standards, and the midnight of moral degeneration deepens. (King, [1963] 1981, p. 60)

Do you believe in absolute truth?

> In our sometimes difficult and lonesome walk up freedom's road, we do not walk alone. God walks with us. He has placed within the very structure of this universe certain absolute moral laws. We can neither defy nor break them. If we disobey them, they will break us. The forces of evil may temporarily conquer truth, but truth will ultimately conquer its conqueror. Our God is able. (King, [1963] 1981, p. 111)

Do you believe open-mindedness is the most important thing in life?

> Jesus reminds us that the good life combines the toughness of the serpent and the tenderness of the dove. To have serpentlike qualities devoid of dovelike qualities is to be passionless, mean, and selfish. To have dovelike without serpentlike qualities is to be sentimental, anemic, and aimless. We must combine strongly marked antitheses. . . . The greatness of our God lies in the fact that he is both tough minded and tenderhearted. He has qualities both of austerity and of gentleness. The Bible, always clear in stressing both attributes of God, expresses his tough mindedness in his justice and wrath and his tenderheartedness in his love and grace. God has two outstretched arms. One is strong enough to surround us with justice, and one is gentle enough to embrace us with grace. (King, [1963] 1981, pp. 18-19)

Do you believe the pink elephants in our field have gone unnoticed?

> Psychiatry helps us to look candidly at our inner selves and to search out the causes of our failures and fears. But much of our fearful living encompasses a realm where the service of psychiatry is ineffectual unless the psychiatrist is a man of religious faith. For our trouble is simply that we attempt to confront fear without faith; we sail through the stormy seas of life without ad-

> equate spiritual boats. One of the leading physicians in America has said, "The only known cure for fear is faith." Abnormal fears and phobias that are expressed in neurotic anxiety may be cured by psychiatry; but the fear of death, nonbeing, and nothingness, expressed in existential anxiety, may be cured only by a positive religious faith. (King, [1963] 1981, p. 122)

Do you agree with these statements? If so, why? If not, why?

- What is liberty?
- What is freedom?
- What is love?
- What is truth?
- What is peace?

How do your responses to these questions impact your work as a therapist, a supervisor, or a professor?

The journey continues . . .

References

American Association for Marriage and Family Therapy (2001). *AAMFT Code of Ethics*. Washington, DC: AAMFT.

American Psychological Association (1998). Appropriate therapeutic responses to sexual orientation in the proceedings of the American Psychological Association, Incorporated, for the legislative year 1997. *American Psychologist, 53*(8), 882-939.

American Psychological Association (2002). Ethical principles of psychologists and code of conduct. *American Psychologist, 57*(12), 1060-1073.

Anderson, D. A., and Worthen, D. (1997). Exploring a fourth dimension: Spirituality as a resource for the couple therapist. *Journal of Marital and Family Therapy, 23,* 3-12.

Andrews, L. M. (1987). *To Thine Own Self Be True: The Rebirth of Values in the New Ethical Therapy.* Garden City, NY: Anchor Press/Doubleday.

Bacon, F. (1998). From Valerius Terminus of the Interpretation of Nature. In *The Oxford Essential Quotations Dictionary* (p. 461). New York: Berkley.

Bergin, A. E. (1980a). Psychotherapy and religious values. *Journal of Consulting and Clinical Psychology, 48,* 95-105.

Bergin, A. E. (1980b). Religious and humanistic values: A reply to Ellis and Walls. *Journal of Consulting and Clinical Psychology, 48,* 642-645.

Bergin, A. E. (1983). Religiosity and mental health: A critical revaluation and meta-analysis. *Professional Psychology: Research and Practice, 14,* 170-184.

Bergin, A. E. (1985). Proposed values for guiding and evaluating counseling and psychotherapy. *Counseling and Values, 29,* 99-116.

Bergin, A. E. (1988). Three contributions of a spiritual perspective to counseling, psychotherapy, and behavior change. *Counseling and Values, 33,* 21-31.

Bergin, A. E. (1991). Values and religious issues in psychotherapy and mental health. *American Psychologist, 46,* 394-403.

Bergin, A. E., and Jensen, J. P. (1990). Religiosity of psychotherapists: A national survey. *Psychotherapy, 27,* 3-7.

Bergin, A. E., Payne, I. R., and Richards, P. S. (1996). Values in Psychotherapy. In E. P. Shafranske (Ed.), *Religion and the Clinical Practice of Psychology* (pp. 297-325). Washington, DC: American Psychological Association.

Berliner, P. M. (1992). Soul Healing: A model of feminist therapy. *Counseling and Values, 37,* 2-14.

Bonhoeffer, D. (1986). *Meditating on the Word.* Cambridge, MA: Cowley Publications.

Boyd-Franklin, N. (1989). *Black Families in Therapy: A Multisystems Approach.* New York: The Guilford Press.

Buchanan, M., Dzelme, K., Harris, D., and Hecker, L. (2001). Challenge of being simultaneously gay or lesbian and spiritual and/or religious: A narrative perspective. *American Journal of Family Therapy, 29,* 435-449.

Byrd, R. (1988). Positive therapeutic effects of intercessory prayer in a coronary care unit population. *Southern Medical Journal, 81*(7), 826-829.

Cade, B. (1997). Directions in therapy. *Contact, 24,* 4-5.

Carter, J. D., and Narramore, B. (1979). *The Integration of Psychology and Theology: An Introduction.* Grand Rapids, MI: Zondervan Publishing House.

Chesterton, G. K. (1900). Article in *The Speaker,* December 15.

Chesterton, G. K. (1906). Article in the *Illustrated London News,* January 13.

Chesterton, G. K. (1908/1995). *Orthodoxy.* San Francisco: Ignatius Press.

Chesterton, G. K. (1928). Article in the *Illustrated London News,* August 11.

Chesterton, G. K. (1929). *The Poet and the Lunatics.* London: Cassell and Company.

Chesterton, G. K. (1930). Article in the *Illustrated London News,* April 19.

Chesterton, G. K. (1936). *Autobiography,* in *Collected Works of G. K. Chesterton,* vol. 16. New York: Sheed and Ward.

Chesterton, G. K. (1936/1966). About relativity. In *As I was Saying* (p. 141). New York: Books for Libraries Press.

Clay, R. (1996). Psychologists' faith in religion begins to grow. *APA Monitor* (August), pp. 3, 48.

CNN (2001a). Bin Laden calls Sept. 11 attacks "blessed terror." Web article, December 27, <www.cnn.com>.

CNN (2001b). Clinton defends pardons, saying individuals "paid in full" for crimes. Web article, January 21, <www.cnn.com>.

CNN (2002). Bin Laden's sole post-September 11 TV interview aired. Web article, February 5, <www.cnn.com>.

Coffey, A. (2001). Spirituality and couples therapy: Ethnographic perspectives from therapy experiences. Unpublished doctoral dissertation, College of Professional Education, Texas Woman's University, Denton, TX.

Cole, B. (2000). The integration of spirituality and psychotherapy for people confronting cancer: An outcome study. Dissertation from Bowling Green State University.

Confucius. From The Confucian Analects, bk. 20:3, iii, as cited in *J. Bartlett's Familiar Quotations.* Boston, MA: Little, Brown and Company.

Crabb, L. (1988). *Inside Out.* Colorado Springs, CO: NavPress.

Cutter, J. A. (1999). Spirituality may help people live longer. Web article, November 17, <www.cnn.com>.

Demling, J. H., Woerthmueller, M., and O'Connolly, T. (2001). Psychotherapie und Religion. Eine repraesentative Umfrage unter fraenkischen Psychotherapeuten.

[Psychotherapy and religion: A survey of northern Bavarian psychotherapists.] *Psychotherapie Psychosomatik Medizinische Psychologie, 51*(2), 76-82.

Dickinson, E. (1872/1960). "A word is dead." In Thomas H. Johnson (Ed.), *The Complete Poems of Emily Dickinson* (poem no. 1212). Boston: Little, Brown and Company.

Dobson, J. (1970). *Dare to Discipline.* Wheaton, IL: Tyndale House.

Dossey, L. Prayer and imagery. Paper at <www.imagerynet.com/atlantis/articles/prayer.html>. Accessed September 6, 2001, and June 9, 2003.

Egan, E. and Egan, K. (Eds.) (1989). *Prayer Times with Mother Teresa.* New York: Doubleday.

Ellis, A. (1980). Psychotherapy and atheistic values: A response to A. E. Bergin's "Psychotherapy and religious values." *Journal of Consulting and Clinical Psychology, 48,* 635-639.

Ellis, A. (1992a). My current views on rational-emotive therapy (RET) and religiousness. *Journal of Rational-Emotive and Cognitive-Behavior Therapy, 10,* 37-40.

Ellis, A. (1992b). Do I really hold that religiousness is irrational and equivalent to emotional disturbance? *American Psychologist, 47,* 428-429.

Emerson, Ralph Waldo (1860). "Worship" in *The Conduct of Life.*

Erickson, E. H. (1963). *Childhood and Society* (Second Edition). New York: W. W. Norton.

Freud, S. (1913/1938). Totem and taboo. In Dr. A. A. Brill (Ed. and Trans.), *The Basic Writings of Sigmund Freud* (pp. 806-929). New York: Random House.

Freud, S. (1927/1961). The future of an illusion. In J. Strachey (Ed. and Trans.), *The Standard Edition of the Complete Psychological Works of Sigmund Freud* (Vol. 21, pp. 1-56). London: Hogarth Press and the Institute of Psycho-Analysis.

Fromm, E. (1941/2001). *Escape from Freedom.* In Leonard Roy Frank (Ed.), *Random House Webster's Quotationary.* New York: Random House.

Gallup, G., Jr. (1999). As nation observes national day of prayer, 9 in 10 pray—3 in 4 daily. The Gallup Organization, May 6, <www.gallup.com>.

Gallup, G., Jr. (2001). Americans more religious now than ten years ago, but less so than in the 1950s and 1960s. The Gallup Organization, March 29, <www.gallup.com>.

Gallup News Service (2001). Easter season finds a religious nation. The Gallup Organization, April 13, <www.gallup.com>.

Gallup News Service (2002). Poll topics and trends: Religion. The Gallup Organization, January 15, <www.gallup.com>.

Gallup Organization (1985). *Religion in America.* Princeton, NJ: Author.

Gallup Poll Monthly (1993). *Report on Trends, 331,* 36-38.

Gartner, J. (1996). Religious commitment, mental health, and prosocial behavior: A review of the empirical literature. In E. P. Shafranske (Ed.), *Religion and the Clinical Practice of Psychology* (pp. 187-214). Washington, DC: American Psychological Association.

Goedde, C. (2001). A qualitative study of the client's perspectives of discussing spiritual and religious issues in therapy. Dissertation. California School of Professional Psychology.

Goodrick, E. W., and Kohlenberger, J. (1990). *The NIV Exhaustive Concordance.* Grand Rapids, MI: Zondervan Publishing House.

Gorsuch, R. (1988). Psychology of religion. *Annual Review of Psychology, 39,* 201-221.

Griffith, J. L. (1986). Employing the God-family relationship in therapy with religious families. *Family Process, 25,* 609-618.

Griffith, J. L., and Griffith, M. Elliott (1992). Therapeutic change in religious families: Working with the God-construct. In A. I. Burton (Ed.), *Religion and the Family,* (pp. 63-86). Binghamton, NY: The Haworth Press.

Griffith, J. L., and Griffith, M. Elliott (1997). Body, mind, and spirit: Therapeutic dialogues. Workshop presented at the Salesmanship Club Youth and Family Centers, Dallas, TX, February.

Griffith, M. Elliott (1995a). Stories of the south: Stories of suffering: Stories of God. *Family Systems Medicine, 13,* 3-9.

Griffith, M. Elliott (1995b). Opening therapy to conversations with a personal God. *Journal of Feminist Family Therapy, 7,* 123-139.

Griffith, M. Elliott (1995c). On not trampling pearls. *AFTA Newsletter,* (Spring), 17-20.

Grimm, D. W. (1994). Therapist spiritual and religious values in psychotherapy. *Counseling and Values, 38,* 154-164.

Haugk, K. (1984). *Christian Caregiving: A Way of Life.* Minneapolis: Augsburg Publishing House.

Hergenhahn, B. R. (1992). *An Introduction to the History of Psychology* (Second Edition). Belmont, CA: Wadsworth.

Hogan, R. (1979). Interview. *APA Monitor,* April, p. 4-5.

Hoge, D. R. (1996). Religion in America: The demographics of belief and affiliation. In E. P. Shafranske (Ed.), *Religion and the Clinical Practice of Psychology* (pp. 21-41). Washington, DC: American Psychological Association.

Holy Bible. (1984). New International Version (NIV) (Reference ed.). Grand Rapids, MI: Zondervan Publishing House.

James, W. (1902/1929). *The Varieties of Religious Experience: A Study in Human Nature* (Revised Edition). New York: Random House.

Jenkins, A. (1990). *Invitations to Responsibility: The Therapeutic Engagement of Men Who Are Violent and Abusive.* Adelaide, South Australia: Dulwich Centre Publications.

Jensen, J. P., and Bergin, A. E. (1988). Mental health values of professional therapists: A national interdisciplinary survey. *Professional Psychology: Research and Practice, 19,* 290-297.

Jung, C. G. (1932/1969). Psychotherapists or the clergy. In H. Read, M. Fordham, and G. Adler (Eds.), *The Collected Works of C. G. Jung* (Vol. 11, Second Edition, pp. 327-347). Princeton, NJ: Princeton University Press.

Jung, C. G. (1954/1968). Concerning the archetypes, with special reference to the anima concept. In H. Read, M. Fordham, and G. Adler (Eds.), *The Collected Works of C. G. Jung* (Vol. 9, Part I, Second Edition, pp. 54-72). Princeton, NJ: Princeton University Press.

Kahle, P. (1995). Practicing psychologists' use of written informed consent forms for therapy: Do mandatory laws make a difference? Unpublished Masters Thesis, Texas Woman's University, College of Arts and Sciences, Denton, TX.

Kahle, P. A. (1997). The influence of the person of the therapist on the integration of spirituality and psychotherapy. Unpublished doctoral dissertation, Texas Woman's University, College of Arts and Sciences, Denton, TX.

Kahle, P. A., and Robbins, J. M. (1998a). Authoring success through competency-immersed therapy. In T. Nelson and T. Trepper (Eds.), *101 More Interventions in Family Therapy* (pp. 440-445). Binghamton, NY: The Haworth Press.

Kahle, P. A., and Robbins, J. M. (1998b). Re-authoring therapeutic success: Externalizing the success and unpacking marginalized narratives of competence. *Journal of Systemic Therapies, 17*(3), 58-69.

Kelly, E. W., Jr. (1994). The role of religion and spirituality in counselor education: A national survey. *Counselor Education and Supervision, 33,* 227-237.

Kelly, E. W., Jr. (1995). Counselor values: A national survey. *Journal of Counseling and Development, 73,* 648-653.

King, M. L., Jr. (1963/1981). *Strength to Love*. Philadelphia: Fortress Press.

King, M. L., Jr. (1963/2001). Letter from Birmingham City Jail, 4/16/63. In Leonard Roy Frank (Ed.), *Random House Webster's Quotationary* (p. 740). New York: Random House.

Kudlac, K. E. (1991). Including God in the conversation: The influence of religious beliefs on the problem-organized system. *Family Therapy, 18,* 277-285.

Lannert, J. L. (1992). Spiritual and religious attitudes, beliefs, and practices of clinical training directors and their internship sites. Unpublished doctoral dissertation, University of Southern California.

Larson, D. B. (1985). Religious involvement. In G. Rekers (Ed.), *Family Building* (pp. 121-147). Ventura, CA: Regal Books.

Leach, L. (2000). Spirituality and healing in medical practice. *Christian Science Monitor,* December 21, p. 14.

Leuba, J. H. (1950). *The Reformation of the Churches.* Boston: Beacon Press.

Levin, J., and Vanderpool, H. (1987). Is frequent religious attendance really conducive to better health?: Toward an epidemiology of religion. *Social Science Medicine, 24,* 589-600.

Levine, J. (1996a). Study: Religion helps smokers kick the habit. Web article, May 15, <www.cnn.com>.

Levine, J. (1996b). Doctors explore use of prayer to fight disease. Web article, July 15, <www.cnn.com>.

Lewis, C. S. (1943). *The Poison of Subjectivism.* Reprinted in Walter Hooper (Ed.), *The Collected Works of C. S. Lewis* (pp. 223-229). New York: Inspirational Press.

Lewis, C. S. (1944/1996). *The Abolition of Man.* New York: Simon & Schuster.

Lewis, C. S. (1947). In W. H. Lewis (Ed.), *Letters of C. S. Lewis.* New York: Harcourt Brace Jovanovich.

Lewis, C. S. (1947/1996). *Miracles.* New York: Simon & Schuster.

Lewis, C. S. (1955). *Surprised by Joy.* New York: Harvest Book.

Lewis, C. S. (1958). *Reflections on the Psalms.* New York: Harcourt Brace Jovanovich.

Lewis, C. S. (1961/1996). *The Screwtape Letters.* New York: Harcourt Brace Jovanovich.

Lewis, C. S. (1963). *A Grief Observed.* New York: HarperCollins.

Lincoln, A. (1866). In F. B. Carpenter, *Six Months at the White House with Abraham Lincoln* (p. 68). New York: Hurd and Houghton.

Lovinger, R. J. (1979). Therapeutic strategies with "religious" resistances. *Psychotherapy: Theory, Research and Practice, 16,* 419-427.

Lu, F. (2000). Religious and spiritual issues in psychiatric education and training. In J. K. Boehnlein (Ed.), *Psychiatry and Religion: The Convergence of Mind and Spirit* (pp. 159-168). Washington, DC: American Psychiatric Press.

Luther, M. (1959). In Ewald M. Plass (Ed.), *What Luther Says,* Volume III (p. 1399). St. Louis, MO: Concordia Publishing House.

Mahoney, M. (2001). Self-care for psychotherapists. A seminar presented at the Texas Woman's University Counseling Center, Denton, TX, October 12, 2001.

McCullough, M. E., and Worthington, E. L., Jr. (1995). College students' perceptions of psychotherapist's treatment of a religious issue: Partial replication and extension. *Journal of Counseling and Development, 73,* 626-634.

McDowell, J. (1977). *More Than a Carpenter.* Wheaton, IL: Tyndale House Publishers.

McDowell, J. (1997). Keynote Address. The Annual Conference of the American Association of Christian Counselors, Dallas, TX, November.

McGoldrick, M., Pearce, J., and Giordano, J. (1982). *Ethnicity and Family Therapy.* New York: The Guilford Press.

McRae, R. R. (1984). Situational determinants of coping response: Loss, threat, and challenge. *Journal of Personality and Social Psychology, 46,* 919-928.

Miller, D. (1996). *The Rants.* New York: Doubleday.

Miller, D. (1998). *Ranting Again.* New York: Doubleday.

Miller, D. (2002). *Dennis Miller Live.* June 28, Home Box Office.

Miller, G. A. (1992). Integrating religion and psychology in therapy: Issues and recommendations. *Counseling and Values, 36,* 112-122.

Milton, J. (1671/2001). *Paradise Regained.* Book iii. Line 329. New York: Penguin Putnam, Inc.

Minirth, F. B., and Meier, P. D. (1978). *Happiness Is a Choice.* Grand Rapids, MI: Baker Book House.

Moon, G. W., Willis, D. E., Bailey, J. W., and Kwasny, J. C. (1993). Self-reported use of Christian spiritual guidance techniques by Christian psychotherapists, pastoral counselors, and spiritual directors. *Journal of Psychology and Christianity, 12,* 24-37.

Nietzsche, F. (1911/1967). *The Will to Power,* Walter Kaufman (Ed., Trans.) and R. J. Hollingdale (Trans.). New York: Random House.

Nohr, R. W. (2001). Outcome effects of receiving a spiritually informed vs. a standard cognitive-behavioral stress management workshop. Dissertation from Marquette University.

Paine, T. (1794/2001). *The Age of Reason.* In Leonard Roy Frank (Ed.), *Random House Webster's Quotationary* (p. 319). New York: Random House.

Pargament, K. I., Olsen, H., Reilly, B., Falgout, K., Ensing, D. S., and Van Haitsma, K. (1992). God help me (II): The relationship of religious orientations to religious coping with negative life events. *Journal for the Scientific Study of Religion, 31,* 504-513.

Patterson, C. H. (1989). Values in counseling and psychotherapy. *Counseling and Values, 33,* 164-176.

Peck, M. S. (1978). *The Road Less Traveled.* New York: Touchstone.

Peck, M. S. (1993). *Further Along the Road Less Traveled.* New York: Simon & Schuster.

Prest, L. A., and Keller, J. F. (1993). Spirituality and family therapy: Spiritual beliefs, myths, and metaphors. *Journal of Marital and Family Therapy, 19,* 137-148.

Propst, L. R. (1980). The comparative efficacy of religious and nonreligious imagery for the treatment of mild depression in religious individuals. *Cognitive Therapy and Research, 4,* 167-178.

Propst, L. R., Ostrom, R., Watkins, P., Dean, T., and Mashburn, D. (1992). Comparative efficacy of religious and nonreligious cognitive-behavioral therapy for the treatment of clinical depression in religious individuals. *Journal of Consulting and Clinical Psychology, 60,* 94-103.

Quackenbos, S., Privette, G., and Klentz, B. (1985). Psychotherapy: Sacred or secular? *Journal of Counseling and Development, 63,* 290-293.

Rauch, C. (2000). Probing the power of prayer. Web article, January 18, <www.cnn.com>.

Rogers, C. (1957). A note on the nature of man. *Journal of Counseling Psychology, 4,* 199-203.

Rogers, C. (1973). Some new challenges. *American Psychologist, 28,* 379-387.

Roosevelt, T. (1910/2001). Speech in Milwaukee, WI, on September 7, 1910. In Leonard Roy Frank (Ed.), *Random House Webster's Quotationary* (p. 630). New York: Random House.

Rose, E., Westefeld, J., and Ansely, T. (2001). Spiritual issues in counseling: Clients' beliefs and preferences. *Journal of Counseling Psychology, 48*(1), 61-71.

Rotz, E., Russel, C. S., and Wright, D. W. (1993). The therapist who is perceived as "spiritually correct": Strategies for avoiding collusion with the "spiritually one-up" spouse. *Journal of Marital and Family Therapy, 19,* 369-375.

Rushdie, S. (1983). *Shame.* New York: Alfred A. Knopf.

Schulte, D., Skinner, T., and Claiborn, C. (2002). Religious and spiritual issues in counseling psychology training. *The Counseling Psychologist, 30,* 118-134.

Segall, M., and Wykle, M. (1988-1989). The Black family's experience with dementia. *The Journal of Applied Social Sciences, 13,* 170-191.

Senge, P., Kleiner, A., Roberts, C., Ross, R., and Smith, B. (Eds.) (1994). *The Fifth Discipline Fieldbook: Strategies and Tools for Building a Learning Organization.* New York: Doubleday.

Shafranske, E. (1995). Religiosity of clinical and counseling psychologists. Unpublished manuscript. In E. P. Shafranske (Ed.), *Religion and the Clinical Practice of Psychology* (pp. 149-162). Washington, DC: American Psychological Association.

Shafranske, E. P. (1996). Religious beliefs, affiliations, and practices of clinical psychologists. In E. P. Shafranske (Ed.), *Religion and the Clinical Practice of Psychology* (pp. 149-162). Washington, DC: American Psychological Association.

Shafranske, E. P., and Malony, H. N. (1990). Clinical psychologists' religious and spiritual orientations and their practice of psychotherapy. *Psychotherapy, 27,* 72-78.

Skinner, B. F. (1953). *Science and Human Behavior.* New York: Macmillan.

Skinner, B. F. (1964/1998). In *New Scientist,* May 21. *The Oxford Essential Quotations Dictionary* (p. 138). New York: Berkley.

Smalley, G., and Trent, J. (1986). *The Blessing.* New York: Pocket Books.

Sollod, R. N. (1992). Letter to the editor. *The Scientist Practitioner, 2,* 33.

Stander, V., Piercy, F. P., Mackinnon, D., and Helmeke, K. (1994). Spirituality, religion, and family therapy: Competing or complementary worlds? *The American Journal of Family Therapy, 22,* 27-41.

Strunk, O., Jr. (1985). A prolegomenon to a history of pastoral counseling. In R. J. Wicks, R. D. Parsons, and D. Capps (Eds.), *Clinical Handbook of Pastoral Counseling* (pp. 14-25). Mahwah, NJ: Paulist Press.

Sue, D. W., and Sue, D. (1990). *Counseling the Culturally Different: Theory and Practice.* New York: John Wiley and Sons.

Tan, S. Y. (1987). Cognitive-behavior therapy: A biblical approach and critique. *Journal of Psychology and Theology, 15,* 103-112.

Tan, S. Y. (1993). Religious values and interventions in lay Christian counseling. In E. L. Worthington, Jr. (Ed.), *Psychotherapy and Religious Values* (pp. 225-241). Grand Rapids, MI: Baker.

Tan, S. Y. (1996). Religion in clinical practice: Implicit and explicit integration. In E. P. Shafranske (Ed.), *Religion and the Clinical Practice of Psychology* (pp. 365-387). Washington, DC: American Psychological Association.

Titone, A. M. (1996). A checklist for exploring spirituality in psychotherapy. *Journal of Texas Assocation for Marriage and Family Therapy, 1,* 25-36.

Vande Kemp, H. (1992). G. Stanley Hall and the Clark School of Religious Psychology. *American Psychologist, 47*(2), 290-298.

Vande Kemp, H. (1996). Historical perspective: Religion and clinical psychology in America. In E. P. Shafranske (Ed.), *Religion and the Clinical Practice of Psychology* (pp. 71-112). Washington, DC: American Psychological Association.

Webster's (1984). *Webster's II New Riverside University Dictionary.* Boston, MA: The Riverside Publishing Company, a Houghton Mifflin Company.

White, M. (1986). Negative explanation, restraint, and double description: A template for family therapy. *Family Process, 25*(2), 169-184.

White, M. (1989). The externalizing of the problem and the re-authoring of lives and relationships. *Dulwich Centre Newsletter* (special edition), (Summer), 3-21.

Worthington, E. L., Jr., Dupont, P. D., Berry, J. T., and Duncan, L. A. (1988). Christian therapists' and clients' perceptions of religious psychotherapy in private and agency settings. *Journal of Psychology and Theology, 16,* 282-293.

Wulff, D. (1996). The psychology of religion: An overview. In E. P. Shafranske (Ed.), *Religion and Clinical Practice of Psychology* (pp. 43-70). Washington, DC: American Psychological Association.

Yalom, I. (1985). *The Theory and Practice of Group Psychotherapy* (Third Edition). New York: Basic Books.

Index

Page numbers followed by the letter "f" indicate figures; those followed by the letter "t" indicate tables.